It's Just Kindergarten... Isn't It?

A Parent's Guide to Kindergarten
Admissions in Alameda County

RISE

Published by Research Institute for Science & Engineering
RISE@ieee.org

First edition: February 2008

ISBN: 978-0-6151-8976-5

Printed in the United States of America

for

Nikki & Max

Contents

Thank You

I would like to thank several people for their help in launching this project. To my husband, John for his patience, sense of humor and ability to help me keep it all in perspective. To my silly munchkins, Nikki and Max, who make me smile, keep me humble and provide oodles of material for this book. To my best friend (since kindergarten!), Pam Molnar, who cheered me on through this roller coaster adventure and who practically dragged me across the finish line. I could not have written this book without her, everyone needs a Pam in their life. To my friend, fellow mom and pizza pal, Julie Jarvis-Reid for her wit, wisdom and encouragement. To Inez Hollander, Lisa Piccione, Joan I. Heller, Ann Gordon, Alyson Spencer and Nicole Westmoreland for taking time out of their busy lives to trim, polish and provide valuable feedback on this project. I appreciate their guidance and thoughtful support. To Laura Lundy-Paine and Greta Wong for providing me with my first opportunity to present my work.

Education is when you read the fine print.
Experience is what you get if you don't.

– Pete Seeger, folk singer, song writer, political activist

You only go around once kid.

– Fred Van Grunsven

An Introduction

Congratulations! Kindergarten is on your horizon. As a parent you have experienced the joy of your child's first smile, first words, first steps. You have also weathered ear infections, teething, sleep deprivation, tantrums, and potty training. Now it is time to add another notch to your parental belt, kindergarten. You may have heard word on the play date or birthday party circuit that there is much anxiety about this whole kindergarten business or better yet, witnessed some of us wild-eyed and frantic parents deep in the throes of tours, applications, interviews, school lotteries, and the like. How you may ask, am I to tackle this beast called kindergarten?

Kindergarten, It's Not Just a School, It's an Adventure

The San Francisco Bay Area is frustratingly unique when it comes to kindergarten. Despite staggering property taxes, your little preschooler is unfortunately not guaranteed a first-rate education. There are some districts where your neighborhood school may be overloaded (i.e., more kindergarteners applying than space available) or you may belong to a district that assigns all schools by a lottery. We are also one of the few areas where you are required to apply (read: compete) to get into private school. When lamenting my situation to a friend back East, she was bewildered by the whole process, "What do you mean you have a lottery for public school?" she said with undisguised horror in her voice and, "Don't you just need to write a check for private school?" If only it were that simple, especially since it is quite a whopper of a check to write.

My Story: Fear Factor

When our number was up for kindergarten, almost daily another blurb in the media would rant about the downfall of our educational system. Word on the street was public schools were not to be considered unless you lived in a wealthy neighborhood that touted the laurels of their public schools and had the home prices to match. I later learned that this was not always true. Other dribs and drabs that came across the kindergarten panic line included private school applications requesting essays on the merits of our little darlings, acceptance rates that rivaled Harvard and Stanford, and tuitions that looked more like a down payment on a house.

I lay awake at night thinking about how I might need to purchase a black board and 5-point restraint system to home school my preschooler who by all intents and purposes had skipped childhood and was now entering adolescence, complete with bossiness, brattiness and outright dig-in-her-heels defiance. How would I be able to get her to sit still and listen to mommy teach her the periodic table? I was having trouble getting her to get herself dressed in the morning.

I realized in my more sane moments that other parents were also feeling overwhelmed. Unsure about where to start, we all knew we were supposed to be doing something and that there were deadlines, but we were unsure if we were on the right track. We also realized that the whole process was ridiculous. I mean come on, it's just kindergarten, isn't it?

Research This

A researcher in my pre-mom days, I decided to roll up my sleeves and collect data. I started by talking to as many parents as I could. I stopped them on the street and peppered them with questions about how they went about their kindergarten search. I eavesdropped on kindergarten conversations in cafes and on playgrounds and I cornered veterans of the kindergarten hunt in elevators. I was greedy for any information I could get my hands on that would explain to me this mysterious and worrisome process. Anything that would alleviate my anxiety and help me sleep at night was hoarded away and jotted down in a notebook. I also surfed the internet on all things related to kindergarten and I made endless rounds of calls to school and district offices.

Looking back on it now I realize that chasing down information, correct information was one of the biggest hurdles. During my foray into the kindergarten world, I found myself frequently frustrated with the overwhelming amount of forms, appointments and deadlines. I often felt like I was trying to learn the secret handshake of the Skull and Bones Society. The information was out there but, I was unsure I had a handle on all of it. Since the time line was intense, I worried that things were slipping through the cracks. Did I visit enough schools? What should I do if I miss the open house at a particular school? Can I get a tour at a certain public school? When are the transfer forms due in Berkeley if I live in Oakland? Is there a right way to fill out the essay questions? How many schools should I be applying to? What do I do if I'm wait-listed at my top school but accepted at another?

The tangible result of my research was a very thick binder stuffed with information on both public and private schools. The process was fruitful but very time consuming. I learned a lot about kindergarten admissions and my hard work paid off since I did find the right kindergarten for my child and our family. Once my daughter was settled into kindergarten, I put my bloated binder on the shelf and patted myself on the back for a job well done. Several months rolled by and lo and behold I noticed a new crop of parents deep in the throes of the kindergarten hunt. Now a seasoned veteran, I adamantly volunteered kindergarten advice and information to parents in those same cafes, playgrounds, and elevators.

Intent & Purpose: What This Guide Will Do

The intent of this guide is to assist you in making a kindergarten game plan by summarizing the various steps in the application process for both public and private schools in Alameda County. Each chapter includes tips and advice that I have gathered along the way. By arming yourself with practical information and a game plan you will be better prepared to make an informed decision on what school or schools are best for your child. For the most part, both public and private schools each have a fairly standard process for kindergarten admissions. This guide provides you with the basic vanilla version, each school will add its own toppings to that basic flavor.

No Guarantees: What This Guide Will NOT Do

Unfortunately, I will not be able to go on tours for you or fill out your transfer forms. However, this guide can help you get a handle on the admissions process, clear up some of the unknowns, and assist (read: guide) you in your quest for a fantastic kindergarten for your child. **This guide does not provide you with individual school recommendations nor does it advocate a particular type of school or education. This guide will also not provide a guarantee that your child will get into the kindergarten you want or that it will answer all of your kindergarten admissions questions.** District and individual school policy, as well as federal and state educational mandates can impact the admissions process. Therefore, you need to follow up with your target schools and districts for the latest forms and updates.

How This Guide is Organized

This guide begins with the basics of how and when to start your kindergarten search in the section entitled GETTING STARTED. From there, we break off into two main sections, PRIVATE and PUBLIC SCHOOL. Each of these sections describes in detail the admissions process for both types of schools. We begin with private school since their admissions process often starts earlier. We reconvene with a discussion of the final decision making process for both private and public school in CHOOSING A SCHOOL. Turn the page, and let's get started.

Getting Started

In this chapter we will discuss how and when to begin your kindergarten search. We start with the basics, kindergarten eligibility, school type and approaches to learning. We will also tackle your family's educational values, commute capabilities and education budget. How your family comes down on these issues will affect which schools you choose to visit, submit applications to and ultimately enroll your child.

Who is Eligible for Kindergarten

Kindergarten as it turns out, is not mandatory in the state of California. Following are the guidelines for both public and private school eligibility requirements.

Public School

According to the California Department of Education website (www.cde.ca.gov):

> Kindergarten attendance is not required by law, but parents have the right to enroll their eligible children in public school kindergarten if they wish. Schools must admit children who have attained legal age. Admission must occur at the beginning of the school year or whenever the students move into the school district. The overwhelming majority of kindergartners must be five years old on or before December 2 of that school year.

In addition, one or both parents or legal guardian(s) must be a resident of the school district. **If your family is homeless your child can still attend public school** *(see* TRANSIENT FAMILIES *in the* PUBLIC SCHOOL SECTION).

Private School

Many private schools require children to be five years of age before they begin kindergarten. The actual cut-off date varies by school. In addition, families are not required to live within a certain district or city to be eligible.

Even though kindergarten is not required, there are libraries full of books and experts a plenty professing the many benefits of kindergarten. Therefore, this subject will not be covered in this guide.

What Types of Elementary Schools are Available

There are three types of elementary schools available in your community: public, private, and home school, following is a brief description of each.

Public School

Your local public school belongs to a school district that is run by an elected school board or in some cases the state. The school district has many functions. One very important function is to determine how schools are assigned. Your public school is determined by your home address. There are four types of public schools, not all are necessarily available in your school district.

Neighborhood: The public school or schools within your neighborhood that your child is eligible to attend. Eligibility is based on your home address.

Magnet:	Public schools that have a particular emphasis built into their curriculum such as art, language, or science. Enrollment is typically based on need as in the case of language school (i.e., bilingual) or a lottery system.
Charter:	Public schools that are run independently of the school board. The educational philosophy or approach to learning is often different from the other public schools within the district. Enrollment is typically determined by lottery.
For-profit:	Public schools managed by private companies (e.g., Edison). The school district pays the private company to hire teachers, manage staff and run the school. Check with individual schools to determine how enrollment is handled.

Please note, a more detailed discussion of the enrollment process for each public school district within Alameda County is covered in the PUBLIC SCHOOL section.

Private Schools

There are two main types of private schools in the San Francisco Bay Area, parochial and independent schools.

| *Parochial:* | These private schools are affiliated with a religious institution and thus, a specific religion is incorporated into the curriculum. Enrollment is determined by application and often an evaluation or interview. Practice of the religion espoused by a particular school is not always mandatory. Each school has its own eligibility requirements however |

priority is given to members of the congregation.

Independent: These private schools are not parochial and as the name says, independently run. In the East Bay there is an alliance of these independent schools called, the East Bay Independent Schools Association (EBISA). EBISA provides a website (www.ebisaca.org) with links to all member schools. Member schools require some of the same forms (e.g., teacher recommendations), and decision letters are all sent on the same date. Enrollment is determined by application and an evaluation or interview.

We will discuss in detail the private school application and enrollment process in the PRIVATE SCHOOL section.

Home School

Children who are home schooled can receive their education in various ways. One or more family members may provide instruction. There are also many home school groups available where one or more parents teach a certain subject. In addition, some school districts within Alameda County provide home school support. Children meet on a regular basis (e.g., once a week) with a teacher, who assigns homework and checks in on progress. There are also many books, websites and computer programs that assist with educational standards and requirements, and instruction of various topics. Furthermore, there are several local institutions that provide classes for home school children, (e.g., Monart, Lawrence Hall of Science). In the Bay Area, we are very fortunate to have many resources and support systems for home schooling.

When to Start: The Drill

One consistent piece of advice I received from kindergarten vets was to start early. Early? I was hoping for something a bit more concrete like, "when the moon is in the second house and Jupiter aligns with Mars." I had fantasies that one of these battle hardy vets would take pity on me, reach into a back pocket and pull out a step-by-step, *How to Get into the Kindergarten of Your Choice Check List.* Alas, that was not to be.

Many of us edgy types turned our kindergarten radar on years before our children were able to properly grip a pencil. Your formal search should **start no later than one year before your child will begin kindergarten.** This time frame applies to both public and private school. Musings on what you want or do not want in a school, and casually checking out schools can start any time beforehand.

How Many Kindergartens

How many schools your family researches, visits, and applies to is a family decision and depends on your situation. I encourage you to cast a wide net. Obviously, the more schools you research and check out, the more opportunities you have for finding the best school for your child. Admissions staff I spoke with recommend:

Visit 8 to 10 schools.

Apply to 3 to 4 schools.

These numbers are guidelines, not gospel. Do not apply to a school that you have no intention of sending your child.

Team Huddle: Pre-Visit Game Plan

Before you start ringing school bells you need to first do some pre-visit homework. I know some of you are thinking, but I do not have time, I need to get out there now and start looking but I encourage you to do a bit of research first. In the long run, it will save you from running willy nilly to schools. Several admissions directors concur, as one put it, "*I know when a parent starts asking me about religion classes--we are not a religious school--that this person has not done his homework.*"

First, discuss with your mates three fundamental issues:

- ✎ Your family's educational values and viewpoints: In what type of school environment would our child thrive?

- ✎ Your family's kindergarten commute capabilities: How far are we willing to walk, bike, bus, BART or drive our child to school?

- ✎ Your family's education budget: How much are we willing to pay for school?

Our goal here is to research and create a list of schools that fall within your philosophical, geographical and financial specifications. These will be your target schools. Keep in mind that at this point, it is ok to not have a clear answer for each of these issues. We will tackle each topic in detail to get you thinking about what works best for your family.

Educational Values and Viewpoints

Your first homework assignment is to get a sense of what your family wants in a school. Discussing the finer points of educational philosophy is not your typical dinner conversation, but a very important one, especially since education has changed a great deal over the past few decades. You will not find any *Dick and Jane* books ("See Jane run. Run Jane run.") in today's classroom. Following is a short list of questions to get you and your family thinking and talking. Keep in mind **the focus should be on what is best for your child.**

My child will thrive in a school that…

    ∗ Is more academic or more developmental?

    ∗ Does or does not give grades?

    ∗ Puts an emphasis on standardized testing or on no testing?

    ∗ Has a more teacher- or student-centered classroom?

    ∗ Has a lot of structure or is loosely structured?

    ∗ Has a more formal or informal relationship between staff and students?

    ∗ Emphasizes and incorporates a certain belief, value or practice into their curriculum (e.g., community service, specific religion, environmentalism, the arts, specific language)?

To help you answer these questions, I have provided a very brief description of some of the most common educational philosophies, approaches to learning and terms you may come across during your kindergarten search. Keep in mind that there are libraries full of books on each of these topics. These descriptions are provided so that you can become more familiar with school jargon.

Academic: Term used loosely to describe schools that put more emphasis on curriculum and less emphasis on social and emotional learning.

Alternative: A broad term referring to schools or educational philosophies that are not traditional. Alternative schools and philosophies include home schooling, charter schools or some independent schools. In some parts of the country an alternative school is one that caters to at risk children or students with special needs.

Constructivist: An approach that emphasizes "discovery learning". Teachers use a hands-on, less directive method of teaching that focuses on students making connections between facts to promote understanding. Teachers ask open-ended questions to promote student thinking and collaborative learning.

Developmental: Term used to loosely describe schools that emphasize a child centered program. Emphasis is on the whole child and educating children at developmentally age appropriate levels. Students are not expected to learn at the same pace.

Montessori: This approach to learning emphasizes students using all five senses to learn. Students learn at their own pace in a structured environment so as to maximize independent learning. Emphasis is also placed on forming communities by grouping older and younger children within a 3 year age range (i.e., 3-6 years, 6-9 years, & 9-12 years) so younger children can learn from their older classmates. Teachers typically stay with the same students for a 3 year cycle.

Progressive: The main objective of a progressive approach to learning is to educate the "whole child" (i.e., physical, emotional and intellectual). Emphasis is placed on "learning by doing" rather than instruction purely from textbooks and students are encouraged toward experimentation and independent thinking.

13

	The classroom setting and relations between teachers and students are less formal.
Traditional:	Traditional schools or a traditional approach to learning is a catch all phrase for those schools that are not progressive or alternative. Classroom instruction is directive, typically teacher centered and text book based. Student achievement is based on a specific set of standards and grades are given.
Waldorf:	This approach to learning emphasizes educating the whole child – "the heart and the hands, as well as the head." A main focus of a Waldorf education is stimulating students' imagination. Electronic media (e.g., television) get in the way of this effort and are therefore discouraged. In addition, teachers ideally will stay with the same group of students throughout their elementary and middle school education.

It is important to note that **one particular school may incorporate many of these approaches.** In addition, each school defines itself in its own way. *School X* and *School Y* may both tout an emphasis on academics and a progressive approach. The curriculum and the actual practice of teaching between these two schools may vary greatly. Therefore, it is imperative that you **ask school staff what they mean and how they put into practice a particular philosophy or approach to learning.** This applies to both public and private schools. Do not assume that all public schools within and outside of a school district are the same. In addition to educational philosophy, you need to consider the staff, the families attending the school, school location and cost. We will discuss these items in subsequent chapters when you begin your school visits. Next let's tackle the remaining two items up for family discussion, your commute and your budget.

Commute Capabilities

Where your child's school is located is not a trivial matter. Once enrolled, you and your child will be making this particular commute for years. You and your family need to put some thought into your commute. Keep in mind that if you find the right school, the commute will be worth it. Discuss the following:

* ✳ Will you choose a school near your home, work, aftercare, or will you consider all or some of these locations?

* ✳ Who will be escorting your child to school?

* ✳ What mode of transportation will you use?

* ✳ Is your child eligible to enroll in more than one school district (e.g., parents each live in different school districts)?

* ✳ Would your family move to get into a preferred school or school district?

Education Budget

Another meaty issue to consider is how much your family can afford to pay for your child's education. Tuition for private school feels more like college rates. In addition, both public and in some cases private schools have additional costs such as before and after care, field trips, school supplies, enrichment classes, busing, and the like. Almost all private schools offer financial aid. At this point, do not cross a school off your list if the price is too high. Talk to admissions staff about eligibility for financial aid and how much is typically awarded. Many private schools have payment plans. We will talk in more detail about financial aid forms and fees in the PRIVATE SCHOOL section.

The K List: Target Schools

Knowing exactly what you want in a school may feel a bit hazy right now, but once you get out there visiting schools, talking to staff, and observing kids in the classroom, you will develop a stronger sense of what you want and don't want — sometimes the "don't" is much clearer. **The very first school to put down on your target list is your neighborhood public school.** Some of you may be shaking your head right now and thinking "no way". I encourage you to first, keep an open mind and second, to use your neighborhood public school as a jumping off point. Next, write down every school that resonates with your newfound educational philosophy, and fits within your commute and budgetary constraints. Add home school to your target list if it is a viable option for your family.

With public schools, do not limit yourself to just your neighborhood school or school district. In other words, if you have heard of a great school across town or in another city, put the school on your list. Families often pull up stakes and move to be in a more desirable school district. You may also have the option of applying for a transfer. We will go over the nitty gritty of transfers in the PUBLIC SCHOOLS section.

At this point in the hunt, keep your list wide open. There will be time for trimming as you gather more information and get out there visiting. Your goal is to come up with a manageable list of schools that you will then start tracking. Log on and check out school and school district websites, obtain application or registration packets, acquire enrollment and transfer forms, and attend open houses and tours. Once a school sparks your family's interest find out the dates and times of school fairs, open houses and tours.

The Devil is in the Details

Many times families get hung up on the details before stepping into a school, "I will not look at that school because it is too big." "I will not consider that school because it has no soccer field." "I will only consider schools that have a middle school." "I will not consider schools with a 'Saint' in front of them because I am not religious." "I will not send my child to public (or private) school."

The tricky part here is to prevent your target school list from becoming too broad or too narrow. One admissions director advises parents, *"Do not set up your limitations in September."* Wait until after the school visits to determine your deal breakers. She compared choosing schools to buying a house. You may not know what factors are important to you and your family, until you get inside and have a look around.

Just the Facts Ma'am

Start your target school list no later than one year before your child will begin kindergarten. If you got an early jump on searching, make sure you update your research if it has been more than an academic year. Keep in mind, schools along with their teachers, principals, curriculum as well as district boundaries change. Most importantly, everyone on the kindergarten hunt needs to fact check. I can not emphasize this enough. Please please please do not rely on what your second cousin's neighbor or anyone else for that matter has said, good or bad about a school. Once you start this game you will find people, including yourself who, have very strong opinions about education and specific schools. What you need to work hard at is filtering out all of that noise.

> **It is imperative that you and your mates check schools out (i.e., school visits and web sites) and you and your mates base your decisions on what you and your mates find out about a school. Do not**

let anyone scare you away from a school until you have had a chance to check out the school yourself.

Remember, different kids have different needs. If the school staff and/or their philosophy put a scare in you, that is an entirely different matter and in that case I suggest you run like your tail is on fire.

A Word About Outliers

An outlier in research is that data point or in this situation a school that does not fit within your constraints. For example, let's say you find a school that just knocks your socks off. It jives with your school philosophy and your budget but is far out of your location constraints. In this case I suggest you keep it on your target school list. Set up a school visit and then decide whether to keep pursuing this school or not. Maybe there is a way to make it work.

Assembling Your A...er...K Team

As you draft your target school list, also think about who can help with your search. Recruiting a teammate to gather and manage paper work or accompany you to an open house or school tour may provide valuable insight and advice. I may be stating the obvious here, but make sure you utilize your team players appropriately. If Uncle Henry is available but lacks attention to detail, better to not have him deal with any paperwork, and if your mother in law is a gem but will soak up all your attention on a school tour, better to leave her at home.

Teaming up with fellow parents who are also on the hunt is another possibility. The advantages are that you can compare notes, share opinions and help each other with remembering important dates, forms and what not. Some of the disadvantages include competition, strain on the friendship, or getting locked into someone else's plan for kindergarten. If your school philosophy or your children's learning styles are different, take this into account, this may or may not be a disadvantage. You can check out what other schools are doing and compare to your target schools.

The Play Book: An Important Note About Notes

Note taking, in my opinion, is a very important part of the kindergarten search process. Therefore, I have included a *Notes* section at the back of this guide. I found that after a couple of visits, the schools became a blur. Ideally, jot down notes as you conduct your pre-visit research and during and right after school visits. You will be at this search for several months and when it is time to fill out the application and make final decisions about where to send your child, these notes will be invaluable.

Get Your Game Face On

It is time to start gathering information so pick up the phone or log onto the internet. Once the information and paper start rolling in, look it over and then put it into one of three categories:

Touchdown: YES – Do your end zone victory dance then mark down all important dates on your calendar and delegate tasks to your team members.

Bench It: NO – If something turns you off about a school, do not punt this one in the recycling bin just yet, for now, bench it. As you begin visiting schools and becoming more school savvy, you may reconsider this crowd. Pull them out before the school tours conclude and applications are due and decide if they are still a no for you. If so, amuse yourself with a spiral toss or punt into the ol recycling bin.

19

Time Out: MAYBE – If you are unsure about a school, mark down important dates on your calendar. Consider attending an open house or at the very least driving by the school to get a better feel for it. If you are still wishy washy, then treat it as a touchdown, for now. Attend all school visits (i.e., open house, school tour), take notes, confer with your team members and from there decide if this school should be benched or not. You will not need to make a concrete decision until it is time to fill out the application.

Organize This

Once you start gathering application packets and forms from schools, you will soon become buried in paper. Keeping it all straight is a quick trip to yawnsville, but a necessary part of your search process. Since the time line is tight and there are many deadlines for just one school, it is important to have a decent if not top rate organizing system. You may need to play around a bit with how to do this but try oh try at the very least to get it all in one place, with important dates written down on a calendar. If possible, delegate this task to an anal retentive team member. Following is a list of the major items you will need:

Calendar: Your calendar will become quite full during the months of September through March. Consider purchasing a special one just for kindergarten, or put it on the main family calendar or just go digital and put it in your *iPhone* complete with bells, whistles and warnings for important dates.

Notes: I have already kvetched about keeping notes. If note taking is not your style, then consider at the very least just jotting down a few words about the school on their flyer or other paper that does not need to be sent in. It could be something as simple as, "lady with orange shirt was very annoying". Knowing she was at School *X* and not School *Y*, the school with the great coffee, Krispy Kremes and vegan power bars, can help you keep all the schools straight.

Filing system: Clear out a file drawer, purchase a binder or dig out a box from the garage, just find a nice roomy place to stash all the paper you will be receiving from schools. I used a binder with nifty pocket dividers that was stuffed beyond capacity by the time I turned in my last form. It served me well and now has a place of honor on my bookshelf. I sometimes gaze upon its bulk with pride and other times, horror.

Questions: This one is easy, I am going to do most of your home work for you on this one. Check out the KINDERGARTEN ADMISSIONS QUESTIONS located at the back of this book. Add and delete items as you go and bring them along to your school visits or when you are chatting on the phone with representatives from the school or the district.

This book: Why not? Reread the sections where you need clarification. Flip to the doodle section and express yourself or send an e-mail to let this author know how this book is working for you. What could be added? What was unnecessary or unclear? What made a big impact? Knock yourself out.

Homework

- ❧ Family huddle – Discuss the three fundamental issues.

- ❧ Research and draft your target list of schools.

- ❧ Assemble your K team.

- ❧ Start contacting target schools.

- ❧ Calendar important target school events and deadlines.

- ❧ Devise filing and organizing system.

You've got your game face on, you have put some thought into what you want in a school, you have a draft list of target schools, and a place to bury…er store all the paperwork. Now turn the page and we will tackle the PRIVATE SCHOOL VISITS.

Private School

School Visits

Visiting schools is many things to many people: informative, engaging, anxiety provoking, inconvenient and at times, down right mind-numbing. School visits boil down to two specific types, the open house, also know as an information night, and the tour. For the most part, private schools use the same basic formula for these visits. I have summarized below what to expect at each event. Keep in mind, each school will add its own spin.

The Open House: Yoo Hoo? Is Anybody Home?

I attended my first school open house with the expectation that it would be like a home sale. The doors would be open and I could wander around from room to room. The real estate agent or in this case the teachers and staff would be on hand to answer questions. Imagine my surprise when I arrived to find a good sized crowd seated in the auditorium, anxiously waiting for the show to begin. Huh? I had left the house telling my husband I would be back in about 30 minutes. I figured I would get there early take a quick peek and be home to watch *Daily Show* re-runs at 8 PM. I did not realize I would be expected to sit through the one hour lecture where staff talked about educational theory and the merits of their school. Following is a summary of what to expect at an open house.

What is an open house?

These events typically last one to two hours and are divided into two parts. The first half typically begins in the auditorium or classroom, where staff deliver a speech about the school and their mission. The second half typically involves a walk through the school. This "walk through" is not to be confused with a school tour (see SCHOOL TOUR description below). In some cases the staff and parents from the school are present.

Why should I go to an open house?

This is your chance to get a first peek at the school, the staff and the facility. More importantly, an open house serves as a prelude to a school tour. This is also an opportunity to talk one-on-one with staff and parents, if they are present. The open house is a great way to begin school shopping.

When do open houses take place?

For the majority of private schools, open houses occur during the fall and winter months, usually when classes are not in session. Some schools offer only one open house while others have more. Check with each school on your list in early fall, to determine when your target schools have scheduled their particular open house(s).

Who should attend an open house?

Bring your fellow parent or a team member along, if you like. Depending on how many of these events you plan to attend, consider dividing them up with your fellow parent. Consider attending the first one or two open houses together. This way you can compare notes.

Who should NOT attend an open house?

Unless otherwise invited, ***do not bring your child(ren).*** If you are expecting your preschooler to "check out" the school at this time, don't. There will be plenty of time for that during the interview. The only exception is if staff invite your child. Babies--the portable sort--who sleep a lot and can be consoled with breast or bottle are usually welcome. Deciding on whether or not to bring your baby, depends on you and your baby, use your best judgment.

How do I sign up?

Just show up at the scheduled start time.

What do I bring?

Bring your mates, questions, calendar and something to jot down notes onto (see NOTES section). Many schools use this event to schedule school tours.

What do I do at an open house?

Arrive promptly, keep your eyes and ears open, and chat it up with staff and other families. Ask questions and scribble down any thoughts, impressions, and unanswered questions. Include your thoughts on the playground, the facilities, the staff, the classrooms, and anything else you can think of. If you like what you see and hear, pick up an application packet and schedule a school tour.

What is an Information Night?

This is another name for open house.

If I am going on a tour, why do I need to go to the open house?

Let's face it, unless you are really into educational philosophy these visits are going to get old pretty darn fast. The speeches, the accolades, and the curriculum can only hold your attention for so long.

After a few visits, the schools start to blend together. However, every contact you have with a particular school, gives you more information about that school. It also provides more face time. *Each contact with the school sends the signal that you are interested.* The staff has more opportunities to get to know you, so when your application comes across their desk, you are not just another name on an application.

What if I miss an open house?

Do not scratch a school off your target list if you miss the open house. Under the best circumstances our lives would be uncomplicated and we would have the time and fortitude to make all of these events. Contact the admissions staff and schedule a tour, then read through all the materials in the application packet before the tour (see THE SCHOOL TOUR). Doing so, should bring you up to speed.

Should I sign up for a tour if I do not have a good experience at the open house?

Deciding to cross a school off your target list and into your *No* pile because of your open house experience should be done with some thoughtfulness. Ask yourself and your mates what it was about this visit that put you off. Keep in mind, the open house is only a first look. Here are some things to consider:

* Was this your first open house? Before crossing this school off your list, get at least one more visit under your belt so you can make comparisons among your target schools.

* Was the school too far away? If so, did you run into traffic or get lost? If this was your first run at the school consider giving it another chance and take a tour.

* Did one person turn you off or was it the entire group? Maybe this person or the group had an off night or their presentation was not up to par. A second look at the school, via a school tour, is a chance to gain more information and make a more informed decision about this school's fate.

* Were you or your fellow parent tired or in a less than sunny mood? Consider giving the school another try after you have recharged your batteries.

* Was it the school philosophy? If you felt you received a clear understanding of this particular school's philosophy and it is not a good fit for your child, then cross it off your list. Otherwise, follow up any vagueness on this issue during the school tour.

* If you can not put your finger on it, but your gut is screaming, "no way" then do not waste your time. However, if you are feeling wishy washy, then schedule the tour.

The School Tour

The school tour is an essential part of the kindergarten search process. Prior to *Le Tour*, log on to the school website, compile a list of questions (see KINDERGARTEN ADMISSIONS QUESTIONS at the back of this guide), read through school literature and mark down all deadlines (i.e., application, teacher recommendations, financial aid, and interview) on your calendar. As with the open house, the following is a basic description of what to expect on a school tour.

What is a school tour?

This is an appointment only type meeting, lasting anywhere from 1 to 1 1/2 hours. Small groups of prospective parents are brought on a guided tour through the school when classes are in session. Typically, admissions staff or parent volunteers serve as tour guide. To accommodate our busy lives, some schools offer some of their tours in the evenings and/or on weekends.

Why should I go on a tour?

This is your one big opportunity to see the school in action. It is your chance to observe the teachers, students, and staff in the school environment. Many private schools require a tour before you can apply.

When do tours take place?

School tours are typically offered during the mid to late fall through early spring. Unlike open houses, these tours are offered on multiple dates.

Who should attend a tour?

Like the open house, bring your team mates. Consider touring on two different dates so as to get another look at the school. Unless invited, **do not bring your children.**

How do I sign up?

Contact the school to schedule a tour. **Do not just show up.** Schools often post tour sign-up sheets at the open house.

What happens on a tour?

Tours are typically divided into three acts:
Act I - Pre-tour gathering and introductions.
Act II - Classroom and school facility visits.
Act III - Re-gathering with question and answer session.

What do I bring?

If possible, bring your mates. Also bring something to write notes on and if possible, prep questions or issues you would like addressed.

What do I do at a tour?

Arrive on time, keep your eyes and ears open, talk with staff and your fellow tourists. Jot down some notes about your thoughts, impressions, and concerns. If you like what you see, pick up an application packet. Unless the staff say otherwise, **do not interact with the teachers or students while in the classroom and do not wander off while on the tour**.

What should I be looking for on a school tour?

Pay attention to interactions among staff and students inside and outside the classroom. Keep in mind that you are getting just a glimpse of the school. Observe and note:

* Conversations and interactions between the staff and you and your fellow tourists. Do they appear friendly, welcoming, stressed out, in a hurry?

* Teacher(s) and other staff interactions with the students, and each other. What do you hear in the hall and on the playground? Is there kindness and respect among coworkers? The students?

* Size and structure of the classroom. Is the classroom adequate in size? Does the room feel over or under crowded? Are the kids allowed to move around or do they spend most of their time sitting? Keep in mind, there will be times when it is necessary for kids to sit quietly (e.g., circle time).

* The student and staff population. What is the age range of the kindergarteners? Are they all six, young fives, or something in between? Is there an even balance among boys and girls? Is the student population diverse ethnically? Economically? Family make up? What about the staff?

* Classroom atmosphere. What is the tone in the room? What are the kids doing? Are the teachers teaching, playing, working on discipline? Would your child be comfortable here?

* The classroom agenda (usually posted somewhere in the classroom). What subjects are taught and are they important to you? Ask about what happens on the other days of the week.

* Transitions. How many classes do the kids have? Are they in the same room all day or do they move to different rooms?

* Art and other assignments posted on the walls. Does every child get a spot or is this reserved for only the star students?

* The student and staff population. Is this a community you want to be a part of? What about your child? Family members?

* Conflicts. You may or may not observe children acting out, but if you do, how does this school handle it? Are you comfortable with how they deal with conflicts? Have students ever been expelled or suspended and if so, why?

* Keep in mind that if you see a difficult interaction (e.g., child acting out, child hurt on the play ground) that these incidents happen at

every school. The important thing to watch for is how the staff deal with these situations.

* Impressions of the building, other non-classrooms (i.e., bathrooms, library, computer lab, auditorium, gymnasium, play ground), outside grounds and location. Do they look cared for or are they in disrepair? Are these facilities being used by the children?

* School parents. What role(s) do parents have at this school? Is volunteering in or out of the classroom encouraged or discouraged?

* Gut check. What is your comfort level here? Are your questions being answered?

These are some things to keep in mind as you tour each school. Just a reminder that an additional list of questions, is located in the appendix, KINDERGARTEN ADMISSIONS QUESTIONS.

If I am going to the open house, why do I need to go on the tour?
Since tours occur when classes are in session, a tour is your chance to try on a school. An open house does not give you this opportunity. Finally, school tours are a mandatory requirement for the majority of private schools.

What if I miss a tour?
Call, apologize and reschedule. If you cannot reschedule, explain the situation to the admissions staff. Tours are almost always mandatory for your private school application to be considered. However, if there are extenuating circumstances (e.g., natural disaster, just moved in from out of town, transferring schools) it is in your best interest to work something out with the admissions staff.

Making an Impression

During my kindergarten search, I frequently struggled with what impression I was putting out there to school staff. Did I appear anxious, aloof, interested, bored, worthy of a slot at their school? I often felt like I was going on a job interview. I dressed carefully, poured over school literature, and gave myself pre-visit pep talks. If I met parents from the school, I especially wanted to make a good impression.

I am also embarrassed to admit that I eyed up the competition with a wary eye. On one tour I enviously watched as a man I like to call *Mr. Pixar* make his way through the school politely chatting with everyone. I had been on the tour circuit for a few weeks and maybe it was the fatigue talking, but I felt this intense level of defeat when Mr. P showed up decked out in his "P" coat. The latest movie logo was subtly stitched on the left breast but, as far as I was concerned it was screaming, "It's *show time* and the perks I can provide are endless."

In my less sleep-deprived, more sane moments, I realized that I was acting like a fool. Do yourself a favor, do your homework, come prepared, and just be yourself. Now, if yourself is something more like Homer Simpson, then when in contact with your prospective schools, try to be more like his next door neighbor, Flanders, without all the diddly diddly doo talk. Here are some things to keep in mind when making contact with the schools. These really are no brainers, but hey, I'm a mother, I like to nag a little.

- ✎ *Do your homework.* Read over school materials and log onto school websites before visiting so you can make the best use of your time and ask thoughtful questions.

- ✎ *Be prompt.* If you are late for a tour, call and either reschedule or surreptitiously join the group.

- *Be respectful.* Teachers work hard to keep everyone's attention in the classroom, so when visiting, do not be disruptive. You are there to observe and unless otherwise invited to do so, do not interact with the students or interrupt the lesson. Teachers may or may not acknowledge your presence as you quietly enter their classroom.

- *Don't brag.* It is ok to be full of pride about your child, but do not cross the line into bragging. For some reason, on all my school visits, some proud parent would share how his child was reading Nietzche, or building a biosphere out of recycled soda jugs in the back yard. This *is* truly remarkable information. However, the message your fellow parents may get is, my kid is brilliant, your's are a bunch of drooling Smurfs. My advice is to save these accolades for the school application form. We will get into how to finesse this in the next chapter.

My Story: Dressed to Impress

I dressed carefully for my first school tour. Since I had spent the past five years with some sort of child induced excrement on my t-shirts and jeans, I was hopeful my pumps and matching outfit would be looked upon favorably by the admissions staff. Surely they would be impressed by my new chartreuse purse and matching sweater, and remember me when selecting candidates for their school. During my pre-tour pep talk, I reminded myself to appear cool and confident even though I felt jittery and clammy. My husband just rolled his eyes and fortunately kept his foolish mouth shut but, who was the real fool here?

A flip flop wearer, I felt like an imposter as I hobbled up to the school determined to appear together enough to get my kid admitted. Hey, I look great, I'm on my best behavior so remember me and take my child, *please*. Unfortunately, I found myself fidgety and bored on many of the school tours. There was much droning on about the merits of each school which at first I clung to. Nonetheless, my eyes along with the schools began to blur. My hearing was also affected since my tour guides began to sound like Charlie Brown's teacher (whaaaa whaa whaa whaa). I don't think I need to draw you a picture of what was happening to those flip flop loving feet, stuffed into pre-pregnancy pumps. After being led into room after room, I composed my face into what I hoped was interest and curiosity. However, I wasn't quite sure what I was supposed to be looking for. Each school had the typical small chairs and tables, curriculum on the board, art on the walls, loft and almost always a couch. I wanted to curl up on that couch and take a nap or get some coffee and chat about the process with my fellow parents. I realized later that these parental interactions could be a double edged sword. In retrospective my time would have been spent more wisely if I had put more thought into what I was looking for in a school, and less time worrying about how I looked.

I Heard It Through the Grape Vine

As you settle in to a routine of visiting schools, you will begin to see familiar faces, fellow parents on the hunt just like you. It is natural, to swap stories and share information about your search with your fellow hunters. These pick up conversations are common throughout parenthood, you share the joys and trials of some stage of parenting with complete strangers on the playground, check out line or in this case, school visits. Rumors, innuendos, conjectures, all sorts of things can come out of people's mouths, including your own. This can be a stressful time and one of the ways to relieve stress is to rant a bit. Trash talking a school, whether you are the trashee or trasher, can be toxic to your search. I urge you not to be sucked in by someone else's rantings or for that matter, be the ranter. Everyone has their own impressions, opinions and kindergarten agenda. **Make sure you do not cross a school off your list because of one or more negative comments you heard through the grape vine.** I think it is important to keep your ears open, but do not take their word as gospel. If there is negative talk about one of your target schools, follow up. If you hear a rumor that the kindergarten teacher is a real battle ax, go check out the school yourself, talk to families who attend the school, do your research and then make a decision. The kindergarten teacher in question may in fact be a real battle ax, or maybe she just rubbed some parent the wrong way. This advice also applies to positive school talk. **Do not apply to a school site unseen.** You need to form your own opinions so that you do not waste your time or money applying to schools you would not otherwise consider.

In my opinion, dated rumors are the most toxic. Finding out that your neighbor, who by the way was searching for a kindergarten three years ago, found the school principal at School X, obnoxious and difficult to work with, is like saying that Madonna is a lame pop artist who really has no talent. But you are talking about the pre-Kaballah Madonna. You are talking about the "La Isle Bonita" and "Like A Virgin", Madonna. Now listen to her latest album and then make a decision. You may still think her music stinks but at least you are listening to the latest stuff and forming an opinion. What I am saying is, schools change like Madonna's hair and style of music. You need to keep up to date on the information, make decisions on what the school is now and not three years ago when a different principal ran the show and the teachers were grumpy battle axes.

Beware Tour Fatigue

At some point during your kindergarten search, you may become worn down and you just can not take it anymore. For the past four weeks you have been out two to three nights visiting schools. The holidays are coming and you have not gotten a thing done. It is all a big blur and the only thing you can think of is, what? Jumping on a plane to Hawaii? Moving to Oshkosh where the public schools are plausible and the living is easy? Crawling into bed and never coming back out? Ah sleep, perchance to dream, of things other than kindergarten. Tour fatigue is common and it hits hard. Your eyes blur, your body aches, and you just do not give a damn anymore...well, you do but you are just so overwhelmed and irritable you say these crazy things. What is a parent to do? Read on for some ideas on how to battle kindergarten search fatigue.

Search Fatigue Busters

- *Delegate.* Tag out and have one of your mates take over.

- *Sensible scheduling.* Look over your calendar and try to spread events out. If possible, give yourself some down time in between visits.

- *Trim your target list.* Be careful here. Tour fatigue can seduce a person into dropping schools like hot potatoes.

Aim to visit eight to ten schools and apply to at least three to four.

🙵 *Change it up.* Devise a way to make the process more enjoyable. Bring a friend, plan something fun after the visit, or work in some rewards for a job well done.

🙵 *Reward yourself.* This search business is exhausting so work in some pay off along the way. Schedule a massage, go for a hike, indulge in a candy bar and nondiet soda, or boogie to some Madonna tunes, just do something to recharge your batteries, so you can get back on the rails.

The point here is to get you back in the game fresh and newly energized. In talking with parents and in my own case, **school visits scheduled later in the season were, if not outright cancelled, met with less enthusiasm.** Viewing schools through what my friend, Julie calls, "the hairy eyeball", will set you up for disappointment. Better to stay fresh and positive, so work in some fun and reward time *during* your search.

My Story: I Got the Rockin' Pneumonia and the Boogie Woogie Flu

Like every year I faced the winter with the renewed hope that my family and I would not succumb to the flu. During the winter of my malcontent...er kindergarten search, I was a woman on a mission. Nothing, not a cold, not even the flu was going to keep me down. So when a cold got in my way, I decided to push through. I would go to bed a tad earlier but, gosh darn it, I was not going to miss the next open house, reschedule a school tour, or miss my self-imposed application deadlines. My cold turned into bronchitis and still I persisted. "What's a little bronchitis?" I thought. I'll catch some extra sleep on the weekends and take my codeine laced cough syrup at bedtime. My bronchitis soon turned into walking pneumonia and still I soldiered on. The last tour I attended, I had coughing spells so intense I had to leave the classroom so I could somehow keep my lungs from spewing out onto the floor. My fellow tourists gave me a wide berth. How wise of them, how foolish of me. My advice to you? Take care of yourself, try to keep your search in perspective, get plenty of rest and if you come down with something, reschedule. You and your fellow tourists will get much more out of the tour if you do.

What's Next?

You are well on your way to finding a school for your child. You are visiting schools and getting a feel for what you like and dislike. Your next major task is to fill out school applications. Turn the page and let's get started.

The Application and Other Important Forms

If you are like me, the idea of filling out forms and applications ranks up there with root canal or a visit to the Department of Motor Vehicles. In this section we will discuss what to expect on the kindergarten application, techniques for completing the essay questions, as well as a brief description and overview of the teacher recommendation and financial aid forms.

Before You Put Pen to Paper: Pre-Application Hoopla

Before you start filling your private school applications, you and your mates first need to decide how many and which schools to apply to. For some of you this may be a clear cut decision, for others, not so clear. Here are some ways to help you fine tune your target list.

How Many Schools Should I Apply To?

As I previously mentioned, apply to a **bare minimum of three schools**. Anything beyond three is your call. Parents typically apply to anywhere from four to six schools. Why three? Applying to one school is risky since everyone who applies rarely gets offered a spot. It is imperative that you have a fall back school, more than one for that matter. The plan here is to avoid having to scramble around in late spring or summer looking for a school, especially since you have done so much work already. Whatever the combination (e.g., three private schools; two public schools and one private; home school, public school and private school) save yourself some grief later on and make sure the bare minimum of possible kindergartens for your child is no less than three.

Post School Visits Target List Tweaking

Trimming your target list can be a challenge, here are some things to consider to make the process easier:

Where Not to Apply

Do not apply to a school you have no intention of sending your child to or one that you have not visited. I am sure this advice sounds ridiculous. You are probably thinking, why is she even telling me this? Why would I waste my time? But tour fatigue, the marketing skills of a fellow team member or a host of other reasons can make us to do crazy things. If this is the only school that sends you an acceptance letter, will you and your mates feel comfortable enrolling your child? If your stomach and your head say "yes", then go ahead and send away. If all systems point to "no way", then do not send in the application.

Trimming the MAYBE Schools

Go through your *Maybe* schools with a keen eye. Look over your notes, talk about the schools with your mates, take a gut check and then determine if you want to submit an application. Move the *Maybes* into the *Yes* or *No* piles.

Application Fees

Each school requires you to send in a fee with your application. The purpose of this fee is to cover the costs of: a) reviewing the applications and teacher recommendations; b) conducting the interviews; and c) sending out the decision letters. These fees can run anywhere from $30 to $100 per school.

Number of Interviews

Once you send in your application, the next step in the process is to schedule an interview for your child. Take into consideration the number of interviews your child can tolerate. Depending on when you turn in your application, the interviews can be scheduled across a number of weeks. The earlier you get your applications in the more time you have to schedule interviews. We will discuss the specifics of the interview in the next section, PRIVATE SCHOOL: THE INTERVIEW.

Filling Out the Application

It is just kindergarten, and yet this application business-- particularly the fees--seems more like college. The applications like the schools themselves vary widely. In addition to the questions about name, address and other basic information, many applications include essay questions. Following are some tips and advice to assist you in completing your applications.

The Whys and What Fors of the Application

The application serves several purposes for you and the schools. The following is a brief summary.

Contact, Background and Diversity Information

Knowing how to contact you is important, as is your and your family members' background information. The private schools loudly tout their mission to provide a diverse community. To accomplish this, schools need information on your ethnic background, family make up, household income, and professional background. Will a school look at just this information and make a decision? Probably not. The other items on the application, the interview, teacher recommendations, and other extraneous information they pick up about you (e.g., letter about you from school alumni) will also factor into their decision.

Competition

As I mentioned at the beginning of this book, some of these schools have acceptance rates that rival Harvard and Stanford. The admissions staff will look over your application and use the information contained within, combined with other information they receive (i.e., interview, teacher references) to determine if your child is a good fit with their school.

Goodness of Fit

The private schools sprinkled around the Bay Area come in many flavors. The staff have a clear idea of what combination of characteristics work well at their school. Therefore, the application will assist the admissions staff in determining if your child is a good fit with their school. For example, if you indicate on your application that your child thrives in a more academic environment, craves structure and would do well with few transitions, then a school that is less structured, less academic and requires its students to move to different classrooms for many of the classes, is not a good fit.

Express Yourself

The open-ended (essay) items are your opportunity to let the school get a better, more complete picture of your child and your family. The admissions staff will use the information on the application to help them better understand your child when he comes in for the interview. If they know from the get go that your child is shy but absolutely adores the color orange, has grandparents who live in Birmingham, and a baby sister named Xena, they can use this information to engage your shy child.

The Guts of the Application

The majority of applications will cover the following areas. Keep in mind each school will have it's own unique style.

- Family background information (names, address(es), occupation(s), list of persons living in your household, marital status of parents).

- Your child's school history (previous and current schools).

- Your child's interests.

- Physical or mental health issues your child has had or is currently experiencing. **It is in the best interest of everyone involved, especially your child, if you are up front and forthcoming with this type of information.**

- Names and professions of specialists your child is currently or has previously seen.

- Comments on how you found out or were referred to the school.

- Open-ended questions about your child, your family, your educational philosophy and how you plan to contribute to the school.

How Do I Tackle This Beast?

When I first looked over the application and saw the essay items, my head spun like I was on Mr. Toad's Wild Ride. I did not have a clue as to how I was going to adequately compose some beautiful prose that would dazzle the admissions staff into accepting my child. Thumbing through my notes, reviewing school literature helped me get a start. As you tweak your essays, keep in mind the following:

- *Don't procrastinate* - I know this is easy to say and it is just common sense. Look over the questions right away so there are no surprises. Mark the due dates on your calendar and get a draft done early. If left until the last minute, filling them out can turn into a nightmare even Freddie Krueger would scream about. More importantly, the sooner you get your applications turned in, the more flexibility you will have in scheduling the interviews.

- *Get to the point* - Waxing on is not a feature here. Get your point across in just a few sentences. Your admissions staff will be most pleased. Remember, they have hundreds of applications to review.

- *Truthiness* - Every admissions director I interviewed emphasized the importance of families being honest and forthcoming about any challenges involving their children (e.g., learning disability, under care of specialist, medical condition). It is in everyone's best interest to make sure the schools your family applies to can address and support your child's needs.

- *Answer the question* - Writing and rewriting your responses is as domestic goddess, Martha Stewart proclaims, "a good thing". Carefully read over your responses and make sure you are answering the question or addressing the issue raised in each essay.

- *Skip the B.S.* - Make your answers honest and about you, not what you think this school wants to hear. Remember, if this is a school you feel good about you should not have to put on a false face.

- *A little flattery is ok* - Show your interest in the school but do not go used car salesman on them. Make it clear you are interested, but try not to sound too desperate, or over-the-top.

☙ *Mention the highlights* - Give a nod to the school's highlights. In other words if their school has won the State Curling Classic six years running and you and your child were bowled over by the clutch extra-end shot executed by the Swedish women's curling team in the 2006 Winter Olympics, then by all means talk this up on your application. However, if you are asking yourself why something as cosmetic as "curling" is an Olympic event, but you love the school for the library and the art program, then talk about the library, the art program and if you mean it, include something about how you and your family look forward to learning more about curling.

☙ *My child is fantastico* - Of course your little one is special and wonderful. Briefly (remember just a few sentences) let them know what makes your sweet potato unique. This will help distinguish her from the herd. My son is a rather adventurous eater. He eats hot dogs with jam, enjoys the occasional peanut butter, jam and ham on rye with mustard on the side for dipping, and a recent favorite, peanut butter and cream cheese on waffles. These tidbits help your child stand out from the pack and in my son's case noted as a, "creative eater".

☙ *Neatness makes a good impression* – I am almost certain you do not want to turn in an application that looks like it was filled out by a twitchy caffeine addict, which begs the question, to type or not to type? My electric typewriter went to Good Will the minute I laid hands on my first laptop computer, an 8086, with a battery pack the size of my forearm, and weighing as much (if not more) as my electric typewriter. Ah the good old days…but I digress. I was taught you type an application because neatness makes an impression. Neatly write in the short items like "Name", "Date", "Address". On a separate sheet of paper type (by computer or typewriter) longer items. If you have more than one typed response, make sure you guide the reader to the appropriate question by including the question number or better yet, include the text of the question followed by your response.

- *Run it by a team member* – Once you have a draft you feel comfortable with, have a team member look it over. This is very important. Do not send in something that has typos or does not make sense.

Taking On the Essay Questions

Since my eldest was going through a...how to put this delicately...a "phase", that only a four year old can dish out, I was in an almost constant state of queasiness during this "phase" of the kindergarten process. Some of you out there look upon the essay items with anticipation. I salute you. For those of you not feeling such bliss, here are some thoughts on how to tackle these items. Keep in mind that these are ideas to get you thinking and writing. **This is not a blue print on how to answer the questions**. Each of the items should have your personal stamp on it. Your mission, if you choose to accept it, is to look over the information below and take away what works for you. Remember your answers should be brief, just a few sentences.

Describe your child.

To help you answer this type of question, think about all the things your preschooler likes to do. Now if your little darling's favorite thing to do right now is draw on the furniture, torment a younger sibling, and defy you at every opportunity then try to remember a time when your weeble was more sweet and less sour. For many kids the favorite's list is long and fluid so stick with just a handful of items. What makes your child stand out from the rest? What is her favorite color, toy(s), activities, food(s). Is she shy? Outgoing? Need a little warm up time? Talk about classes she is currently or has previously taken (e.g., martial arts, dance, piano, etc.) or include something about her favorite activities at preschool, day care or home.

What are you looking for in a school? or Why are you applying to our school?

Talk briefly about what kind of education you want your child to receive. Are you looking for a school that is more academic, developmental or a mixture of both? Work in how your child would thrive in this kind of a program. It could be something as simple as stating that her current preschool is more developmental and she thrives in this type of a program because _____ [you fill in the blank]. Include something about what you hope your child will gain from going to this school, such as, a safe, happy place to grow, or a solid education that will lead to an ivy league school, or a place where she can indulge in her love for art, science, math, or a second language. Talk about how you learned about the school and what drew you to it. State why this school stands out from other schools you have toured. If you know other families who attend the school mention them here.

What can you contribute to our school?

List and briefly describe volunteer work you have done at your child's preschool. Make sure you include activities like being a chaperone on field trips, making snack or reading to the class at circle time. Briefly talk about activities you would like to help with at this school. Include skills from your professional background that you could share with the school. Be real here. For example, if you love to sew or are into the theater, mention that you would enjoy helping out with the school play. If your professional and personal background do not necessarily fit with what the school offers, just letting them know that you are willing to roll up your sleeves and help out in anyway you can is good too.

Whoa Yes, Wait a Minute Mr. Postman

Popping your master piece in the mail is fairly easy but consider hand delivering your application. Better yet, consider having your child come along for the delivery. It is another chance to get a look at the school and a relatively easy introduction for your little one. Just make sure it is a good time of the day for you *and* your child, not to mention the school. Visits during school arrival and dismissal times will be chaotic for not only you but the staff. Try for mid morning or early afternoon. This is optional, hand deliver only if it works for you.

My Story: I'm Walking on Sunshine, Whoa Oh

The euphoria I felt upon finishing my first application was too good not to share. I wanted to high five everyone I saw and in retrospect I guess I was expecting a balloon drop and confetti cloud to go along with my excitement. I mean come on, I poured my soul into this application. Verbs were chewed and rechewed, I dithered over punctuation, and my thesaurus still simmered from overuse. However, the person working the office apparently was not in on my little drama. She kindly smiled as I merrily greeted her, and said thank you as I happily turned in my application forms. She then proceeded to unceremoniously toss my master piece on to a pile of already received applications. Sigh. I figured a victory lap around the school grounds, with arms raised over my head as I hooted in glee would not help push my application into their *Yes* pile. So, I contained myself and did a little victory dance in the car to some hopelessly lame 80s music-- *I'm walking on sunshine, whoa oh. And don't if feel good?*

Bribes, Brown Nosing & Other Annoying Behavior

Letting the school staff know that you are enthusiastic and interested in their school is a good thing. Coming across as a bothersome pain in the...er...neck is not a good thing. You want the staff to smile when they think of you, not sprint away in terror as they see you approach or groan as they listen to your thirteenth voicemail of the day. I realize these can be anxious times, and many of us are not at our best when feeling the pressure. Following are some behaviors we can all fall prey to. If you see yourself in some of these personalities, do your best to ratchet it down a notch or two.

Brown Noser: As we all learned during our school days, this annoying sucking up type of behavior will not gain you many points. Admissions staff have seen it all, so yes, show interest but avoid the feigning and the fawning.

Braggart: Of course your child is magnificent but keep in mind all the other parents think their child is too. It is ok to be positive about your child, just no soap box lectures on how you have bred your very own Einstein with hints of Picasso and Mozart thrown in. The admissions staff will have their opportunity to soak up your prodigy at the interview.

Stalker: I encourage you to ask questions, request information and follow up with the admissions staff. However, obsessively calling the staff or repeatedly showing up on school grounds will not help your case.

Über Achiever: The Über Achiever takes it several steps beyond the over achiever; this person takes it waaaaay over the top. This chap is not content to just fill out the application form. This parent includes a photo album or DVD movie of his child's life or writes a 10 page dissertation on how this school will provide the necessary and appropriate educational experience for his child. If you see yourself going in this direction stop and take several steps waaaaay back. Remember it's just kindergarten.

Teacher Recommendations & Financial Aid

Teacher recommendations and financial aid forms are also part of the application process. Financial aid is optional, teacher recommendations are not. Please note, the deadline for teacher recommendations and financial aid may differ from the application deadline.

Oh Teacher, I Need You

Teacher recommendations are a very important piece of the application process. Following is a summary of the whys and what fors of these recommendations. Keep in mind your target schools may add some of their own requirements:

What is a teacher recommendation?
There are typically two types of teacher recommendations, the recommendation letter or form. Each school will specify what format they require:

* *The Letter* - The recommendation letter is just a free style letter your child's teacher(s) will draft about your child, highlighting his school behavior. It is similar to a job reference letter.

* *The Form* - The recommendation form requests the teacher(s) to answer specific questions about your child (e.g., *ability to work and play cooperatively, focus on a task, areas most needing support or adult intervention*). The East Bay

Independent Schools Association (EBISA) recommendation form is fortunately the same for all of their over 40 member schools (see www.ebisaca.org). In other words, your teachers will only need to fill out the form once and then photocopy and send it to EBISA schools on your target list.

Why are teacher recommendations important?
Your teachers have a unique window into your child's school behavior. This information weighs heavily in your application (see the example recommendation form questions listed above) therefore, it is imperative that you put these forms high on your priority list. **It is easy to lose track of this part of the process since you are not responsible for drafting the recommendation letter or filling out the recommendation form.** Calendar their due dates and keep track of their progress as you are doing with the application and other necessary forms.

What do I need to do to get the teacher recommendations completed?
Your child's preschool or the teachers themselves may have a process they like to follow so first check with them. If there is no set procedure then create a packet of materials for each school and each teacher completing the recommendations. Note, some schools require recommendations from one or more teachers.

What should I include in my teacher recommendation packets?

* Name of the school applying to.

* Teacher recommendation due date

* Addressed (target school address) and stamped envelope.

* Recommendation form (if required by target school).

When are teacher recommendations due?

The due dates for teacher recommendations vary among the schools therefore it is important that you calendar these dates. **It is good form to get your teacher recommendation packets or whatever materials needed by your teachers, at least one month before they are due.** Your preschool teachers have many of these recommendations to complete. You want them to look favorably on your little one, not with a jaundiced eye because their adults got forms to them late and are now breathing down their neck to get the darn thing done. Check in periodically to see if they have been sent but try not to nag. A polite, "Do you need anything else from me to get those recommendations out the door?" may be all you need to remind them.

Why are teacher recommendations confidential?

The application and interview provide only a snapshot of your child. The admissions staff want feedback on how your child behaves in a school environment. **Most schools will not accept a teacher recommendation if it is turned in by you.** Unless otherwise indicated, have your teachers mail appropriate documents directly to the school (see TEACHER RECOMMENDATION PACKETS description listed above).

What if my child is currently not enrolled in preschool?

Ask teachers from classes your child has or is enrolled in (e.g., dance, gymnastics, martial arts, etc.)

If this is not a possibility, contact your target schools and ask how they would like you to proceed.

What do I do if my teacher recommendations have not been turned in on time?

Let's face it at this stage in the game you will be trying to stay on top of a lot of paperwork. The following are some tips on what to do:

* *You Dropped the Ball* - You may have written down the wrong due date, did not include the stamped and addressed envelope or the form. This is easy to do so apologize, forgive yourself, and then get done what needs to be done, fast. Double check all other outstanding teacher recommendation packets to make sure they are complete, correct and on time.

* *Teacher Dropped the Ball* - If one or more of your teachers has dropped the ball, try to find out why and then work to get it fixed. Did they forget the due date, lose it on their desk or something else? Remain calm (remember they are going to be making a recommendation for your child) and talk with your teacher about how you can get this done. Contact the admissions staff and explain the situation. Try to be diplomatic here. It is not a good idea to trash a teacher to a potential school. In some cases, they may contact the teacher directly and either ask them to send the letter or form or instead have a phone conversation that would take the place of a written application. Just make sure that you have done your part in the process, that is, delivered your complete teacher recommendation packets to your teachers no later than one month before they are due. It would be grossly unfair to harp on a teacher if

you only gave her the packets shortly before they were due.

    ✳ *Unknown Forces Have Conspired Against You* - If one or more recommendations disappeared into thin air contact your target school and ask them how to proceed. Do some detective work to see if you can locate the darn thing.

Whatever the reason, it is imperative that you keep the lines of communication flowing between you, your target schools and your teachers. Ask your target schools how they would like you to proceed with a late teacher recommendation. Would a quick call to the preschool teacher by the admissions staff suffice or would it be possible to have the teacher do or redo the recommendation ASAP? Would it be better to get a recommendation from another teacher or stick with this one? The schools tend to be reasonable about this, especially if you keep your cool and are showing that you are rolling up your sleeves to get the job done. It also is another opportunity for you both to learn more about each other. Is your target school easy going about this snag or are they autocratic and demanding?

Financial Aid Forms

The cost of private school is staggering, there is no denying it. Tuition for private school is in league with many colleges and universities. To make things even more exciting, tuition rises every year. How much it increases depends on the school. If you are eligible, financial aid can take the edge off. If you are unsure if you are eligible, then fill out an application. What do you have to lose? I encourage you to talk with the admissions staff about tuition. According to the admissions directors I spoke with, financial aid awards vary from year to year. It depends on the number of families making a request, the amount granted to each family and how much money the school has to give.

Almost all private schools grant some type of financial aid. Typically, it is not awarded to every family. The Catholic Diocese of Oakland, which has schools throughout Alameda and Contra Costa counties, provides tuition assistance from two sources:

- Family Aide – Catholic Education (FACE), an internal diocese funding source.

- Bay Area Scholarships for Inner city Children (BASIC) an external diocese funding source.

Schools belonging to the East Bay Independent Schools Association (EBISA) each generate their own funding. EBISA schools require families to complete two types of financial aid applications. Decisions about who qualifies for financial aid and the amount granted are made by your target schools and based on the information provided on the following applications:

School & Student Service for Financial Aid (SSS) Application

The SSS is provided by the National Association of Independent Schools (NAIS). The NAIS reviews and generates a Parents' Financial Statement (PFS) based on the information provided in your SSS application. Your PFS is then sent to your target schools for review by the financial aid staff. SSS applications are available from those schools that require them and are also on line at: *https://sss.ets.org/*. This website is a great resource. It answers common questions and provides an online application. Some schools waive the SSS application fee for financially disadvantaged families. Contact your target schools to learn more.

**Keep in mind the deadline for <u>receipt of your PFS</u> is typically different from your admissions applications. Do not confuse this date with when you need to complete the SSS. Remember you need

to complete the SSS BEFORE the PFS can be generated. The deadline you need to be concerned with is when your target schools need to receive the PFS.**

At the time of publishing, the NAIS website stated,

> *Please allow two days for SSS to process your Online PFS. The schools you indicate on your PFS will be able to view your Online PFS within two days. Please allow 7 days for SSS to produce and mail the Report of Family Contribution (RFC) to the schools listed on your Online PFS and to you if you indicated a Report of Family Contribution (RFC) Family Report on your Online PFS.*

School Financial Aid Application

Each school has its own financial aid forms. These documents are included in your application packet and in some cases can be downloaded from school websites. These forms typically require copies of federal tax returns from the current and/or previous year(s). As opposed to the SSS, you will be responsible for delivering this form to each of your target schools. **Note, the deadline for your target school's financial aid application can differ from the SSS and your child's admissions application.** Contact your target schools to learn more about funding sources and the financial aid application process.

What's Next?

Your paper work is complete and sent in, woo hoo! Take a victory lap. Your next big task is to schedule and prepare for your child's interviews. Turn the page and we will get you and your family prepped.

The Interview

How, you may ask, does one conduct an interview with a preschooler? Before I got to this point in my kindergarten search, I imagined school staff sitting my child down at a conference table and conducting a job-like interview. In my more freaked out moments I would take this a step further and envision my child in an interrogation room with *24*'s *Jack Bauer* demanding that she recite the alphabet in French and do long division. Fortunately, the actual interviews are not so intense. For the most part interviews are a kid and parent friendly event. We will get into the details of the kindergarten interview but first, if you have not yet scheduled your child's interviews, crack open your calendar and hop to it.

Scheduling Interviews: It's Just Another Manic Monday

How you schedule your child's kindergarten interviews depends on you and your child. Some families just want to get it over with as quickly as possible. Others find that scheduling the interviews across a few months makes it easier to swallow, and still others put it off for as long as possible. Whatever your situation, call early so that you have a better chance of getting the schedule you want. Note, setting up appointments earlier in the season gives your family some leeway in case you need to reschedule. Let's face it this whole process takes place during cold and flu season.

The Whys and What Fors of the Interview

During the interview school staff will observe and interact directly with your child. As with all things kindergarten, each school applies its own unique spin. Some schools take a more serious tone while others are more light-hearted about the process. For all schools, the interview serves to answer two big questions:

> **Is this child ready for kindergarten?**
>
> **Is this child a good match for our school?**

Note, some schools refer to this phase of kindergarten admissions as the *evaluation*.

The Mechanics of the Interview

A typical kindergarten interview is comprised of four main parts: warm up, separation, evaluation and reunification. The entire process takes anywhere from 1 to 1 ½ hours. Some schools prefer to meet one-on-one with your child, but the majority of schools conduct group interviews. Following is a general description of what typically takes place during an interview. Talk with admissions staff to get a more concrete sense of how their school handles the interview.

Warm up

> The warm up takes place before the actual interview. It is a time when you and your child can get acclimated and comfortable. If possible, use this time to explore the room with your child. Try to keep the mood light and fun.

Separation

The separation portion of the interview is when either the parents or the children are asked to leave the room. This is the most anxious part of the process. Some schools will have the children line up and walk over to another room sans parents, while others have the parents say their goodbyes and leave the room. We will discuss how to prepare you and your child for this separation in the section, PAVING THE WAY FOR A SMOOTH SEPARATION.

Evaluation

For group interviews, the evaluation portion of the interview typically takes place in one of the classrooms. During the evaluation the staff interact with your child and if present the other children. They engage them in various activities and once complete, reunite them with their adults.

Reunification

Once the evaluation is over you will be reunited with your child. I encourage you to celebrate in some fashion, regardless of whether or not it went well. Setting a precedent for a post-interview fun activity may be just what you need to get your child in the right frame of mind for the next interview.

What's the Buzz? Tell Me What is Happening

In some cases, finding out about what goes on during the evaluation is like trying to crack the Da Vinci code. Some schools are very open about what goes on, while others are down right cagey. Here are some of the activities that commonly take place during the interview. I realize I sound like a broken record here but this is general description. Directly ask the staff what happens during the evaluation.

Ice breakers: What's a nice kid like you doing in a place like this?
The goal of the ice breaker is to get the kids comfortable and also to observe how they handle the situation. The standard ice breaker is most often dealt with in circle time. Some examples of circle time ice breakers include asking each child to guess which type of animal will be coming in for a visit, singing a song, or sharing names, ages or favorite colors.

Can you paint with all the colors of the wind?
Staff ask the kids in small groups or individually, to draw a picture. This activity is rich with information. Some schools request a specific type of picture such as, a picture of yourself or your family. Other schools ask the kids to draw whatever they want. By looking at how and what your child draws the school can evaluate several things: How does your little one hold a pencil? What is the drawing of? How detailed is the drawing? Are they using different colors? If so, do they know the names of the colors?

We all live in a yellow submarine.
How your child interacts with the staff and his peers is another component of many interviews. The staff will observe how your little guy separated from you, how he behaves in circle, and how he plays with the other kids in the room.

You put your left hand in you put your left hand out.
Gross motor skills, that is, your child's physical abilities have also been included in some interviews. Hopping on one foot, playing *Simon Says*, or other movement type games are used to look at how well your child listens to direction, how well she moves physically, and also allows kids to burn off some energy.

Conjunction junction what's your function?

Some schools will also ask the kids questions about what they know (e.g., counting, reciting the alphabet, naming colors). I am not trying to freak you out here and have you start drilling your kids on multiplication tables. All pre-Ks need to know certain basics before starting kindergarten. This activity allows the staff to get a feel for what your child knows. The library, book stores and web are chocked with books and information on what kids need to know before they start kindergarten. Again, I encourage you to ask your target schools what types of questions they will be asking your child and what type of information your child will need to know to take part in the interview.

I'm as free as a bird now.

Since the room is filled with toys and school materials the kids are sometimes allowed to just roam when not sitting in circle or being asked to interact with the staff. The teachers will then observe how your child behaves. Is he at the door waiting to leave? Did she sit down with some building blocks and start creating a master piece? Is he playing dress up with some of the other kids? Is she swinging from the loft and not listening to the requests of the teacher to, "Come down from there please." Is he organizing a mutiny and planning to rush the door?

The Interview: Preparing Yourself

For many of us, the interview is the most worrisome piece of the kindergarten puzzle. It is the part where we as parents, have the least control and our children and the school staff have the most control. That said, let's get a few things out on the table. First, these schools have been doing interviews for many years, and as I mentioned before, they have seen it all.

They have dealt with shyness, chattiness, tantrums and all sorts of "exciting" behaviors our little pre-Ks can dish out. Your mission is three-fold:

* *Talk to the admissions staff.* Find out as much as you can about how each of your target schools conducts the interview.

* *Be cool.* If you take events like this in stride, hats off to you. If you are more edgy like me, work hard to go zen and stay in this happy little place until your child leaves the room for the interview. If it helps, take a deep breath or two and remind yourself that in another couple of months this will all be over. See PAVING THE WAY FOR A SMOOTH SEPARATION for more details.

* *Prepare your child.* The trick here is to not over prepare. Below I have compiled some tips and advice for you and your mates to ponder.

Preparing Your Child: *But I Don't Wanna Go!*

Prepping your child for the interview can feel like a walk on ye old tightrope. Too much information can over load your little dude, while just showing up at the interview with no heads up for your child can back fire too. One piece of advice I received from a school administrator and kindergarten interviewer, was to tell my children we were going to visit the school so they could check it out. The idea here is to let them think they are part of the process, but not the final decision makers. Instead, make it sound more like a play date. Keep it casual. Something along the order of,

> *On Saturday we're going to check out Mary Poppin's Supercalifragilisticexpialidocious Academy. It has cool toys and kids your age will be there. I'll need to sit in on a boring meeting with the other parents for a while, but you can keep on playing with the toys and other kids. There*

will also be some teachers there and they will have some fun games to play. After, how about we _____ [insert one or more of your child's favorite activities].

Paving the Way for a Smooth Separation

Here are some more tips on how to prep your child for the interview. Obviously you know your child best so use what you can to make your interview run as smoothly and as stress free as possible.

* *Keep it simple.* - Over explaining the process is only going to confuse your child. My advice is to keep it simple and try not to go into too many details that could overwhelm your child.

* *Keep it casual.* - If you are feeling uptight and anxious, they will smell it and most likely react. I know this is hard but try your best to play it cool. Avoid the high pitched sing songy I'm-trying-to-talk-you-off-the-ledge voice.

* *Pre-interview school visit(s).* - There is nothing like a little reconnaissance work when it comes to preparing everyone for the interview. Taking your child to the school to drop off your application or to just drive by and see the kids playing on the playground, is a good way to get your child prepared for the upcoming interview.

* *Avoid the rush-rush.* - Give yourself plenty of time to get to the school so you and your child have time to get acclimated. Walk around the grounds (a good way to burn off some energy) or wander through the school and look it all over once again. This is another chance for you to get a feel for the school, and most importantly, to help your child get comfortable.

* *Don't over prepare your child.* - Daily drills on interview preparation puts too much pressure on you and your child. If you want to make sure your child knows some basics, consider making these activities into a game. Sing the alphabet song, play games like *I Spy* to identify colors and numbers and provide gentle reminders about playing nice and listening to the teachers. The point here is to keep it light and fun. Remember, these interviews are more like a play date, not an SAT exam.

* *Don't over sell.* - Talking up the interview or the school for that matter, too much can make certain independent minded little ones kick up a fuss. In other words, you want me to like this so I won't.

* *Solo parenting.* - Having one parent take on the interview has several advantages. It may make it less of a big deal if only one of you attends. Also, if you are concerned about your child being clingy, consider having the parent who is clung to least, accompany your child. This may make the separation phase go more smoothly. The other parent can stop by after separation and enjoy the thrill of reunification and post-interview fun.

* *Do not bring toys from home.* - Your child's fellow interviewees may want to get their hands on your child's cool toy. It is best to leave toys at home or in the car and avoid any potential scuffles.

* *The boring meeting.* - At one school the admissions director told the kids that their parents were going to go across the hall to a really boring meeting. She told the kids they would get to stay and play with the toys and then have a snack.

* *Schedule interview with a friend.* - If you know another family who is applying to the same school, consider scheduling your kids' interviews at the same time. Knowing a school mate or friend will be there will make it more like a play date.

* *Focus on the future.* - Promising a fun activity after the interview is another way to gain some cooperation from your little tyke. In fact, if you focus your excitement on the post-interview activity (*I can't wait until Saturday when we can go to the zoo. We just need to swing by The Mary Poppins Supercalifragilisticexpialidocious Academy for that boring meeting and then we can go.*)

* *Reschedule.* - Rescheduling an interview should occur only if your child is sick, there is a family emergency, the staff request it, or your child has a core melt down AT the interview. We all have bad days and sometimes the situation just screams that this is not our day. If this should happen, consult with the admissions staff about rescheduling.

My Story: It's Just a Flesh Wound

I figured my second child's kindergarten interview would be a cake walk. We knew what to expect and we as a family, were a known product to the school. Still, I gave him the "boring meeting" speech and a brief run down on what would happen. My only concern was that the interview was scheduled for 3:00 PM, a time I refer to as cranky hour, aside from that, I was rather *que sera sera* about the whole thing.

On the drive over, my son was atypically psyched for this time of day. He was chatty and excited about getting to play at his big sister's school. Woo hoo I thought with a smug smile. I pulled into our parking space and in his excitement my little dude jumped out of the car throwing over his shoulder, "I'll meet you on the sidewalk Mom." A second later the door slammed immediately followed by a pain-filled screamy moan. My heart stopped, my stomach dropped. I scrambled out of the car only to find my sweet boy curled in on himself. He was breathing hard, his eyes sparkling with tears ready to spill.

It was clear that he had just slammed something in the car door. A quick inspection confirmed he had smashed his right thumb. Before my eyes, it was turning a bright sickly blue. My stomach took another dive and my heart rate was at aerobic capacity. I knew he needed something to ease the pain and fast. Accompanied by some horror movie screaming, I carried him into the school and a quick visit to the office for some ibuprofen. All thoughts of the interview gone, we found a quiet corner to sit and get our equilibrium back.

As our little drama was playing out, my fellow parents were arriving with their interviewees. They were sympathetic, thinking that my guy was freaking about the interview. The admissions director reassured me that we could reschedule. The blue fingernail was my signal that we would definitely be leaving soon. Twenty minutes from impact, my brave little guy, who can not pass up a toy filled room, was on his feet working it. Although he was not as chatty, he did insist that he was ok to go play with the kids and teachers in the other room. After that adrenaline rush *I* did not want to let him go. I had not recovered yet, but what's a mom to do? As he lined up to leave it was I who got teary eyed and did not want to separate. I wanted to kick up a fuss, play velcro leg and cry *No!*

What did I learn from this little adrenaline laced scenario? First, good ol Murphy and his law can pop up at the most interesting of times. Second, by keeping my cool (on the outside), I'd like to think it made it easier for my son to bounce back. Third, the interview was scheduled early in the interview season, so I had the fall back of rescheduling. Fourth, by arriving early my son had ample time to recover, work over the room, and take part in the interview. Fifth and final, take Vicki Iovine's advice (author of the *Girlfriend Guides* and girlfriend to one and all), and have my children touch their nose with one hand while they close the car door with the other. Amen.

The Post-Mortem: Tell Me What Happened

You made it. You and your family have been working towards this moment for months and now it is time to celebrate good times, come on. If you are like me, at some point during your post-interview victory lap, you start to wonder (worry?) about what actually went on during the interview. Did your little pre-K take part in all the activities and dazzle them with her impeccable manners and knowledge or did she stand by the door and refuse to talk? You need a little color commentary on what actually happened in that interview room and quizzing your child is coming up with nothing, nada. Since the interview plays a big role in the application process, I wanted to know if we had a chance at this school or if I needed to call and explain, reschedule or worse yet, apologize. I quizzed both my kids about what happened during the interview and came up with little information. If you have got a tight lipped little tyke, here are some tricks you might try.

- *Give 'em a break* - Sometimes they just need a break and would be more willing to talk about interview details later. Focus on other activities right after the interview and later in the day or in a few days they may talk about what happened.

- *Don't know much about history* – You can also try the messed up facts trick so that your child will correct you on what actually took place. *I heard you got to sit in circle and see a turtle. No Mom, it was a guinea pig.*

- *Bedtime story* – There is something about that sleepy time right before bed when you snuggle and talk to loosen those lips. Wait until bed time to ask a question or two.

- *Call in reinforcements* – Have a fellow parent or family member do some innocent questioning. A call to a grandparent or other favorite relative or friend about the big day might get your little one talking.

- *Let it go* – Your child may or may not open up and if so, then call the admissions staff or a parent with a fellow interviewee to see if together you can piece together what happened and how well it went.

What's Next?

You have come a long way and you are making your way to the finish line. If you have not already done so, it is time to get acquainted with the admissions process in the public schools. Turn the page and let's get started.

Public School

Registration and Enrollment

Many families take a more laid back approach to enrolling their children in public school and in many school districts the process is rather painless. There are no essays to complete as with private school. However, public school does come with its own laundry list of requirements and forms. In this section we will discuss the ins and outs of kindergarten registration and enrollment in the Alameda County public schools. We will first go over the basics of kindergarten admissions followed by a series of QUICK FACTS pages for each school district within Alameda County.

As with private school, this guide will cover the basic information, the vanilla. Unless mandated by the federal or state government, each school district has it's own unique way of handling certain parts of the registration process (e.g., forms, deadlines). Therefore, you and your kindergarten search mates need to follow up with each of your targeted schools and districts. Throughout this section, I have included several 🦌 ALERTS to get your attention. These 🦌 ALERTS provide vital information unique to your school district and will most likely impact your kindergarten registration.

As I kvetched throughout the private school section, it is imperative that you do your homework, stay on top of the deadlines and complete your registration paper work early. **Unfortunately, living in a certain neighborhood or school district, is not a guarantee that your child will be enrolled in your neighborhood school.** Yes, you heard me correctly.

Your child may be eligible to attend a particular neighborhood school, but your child unfortunately, is not guaranteed a spot at this school. This situation is referred to as *overload* and we will discuss this nasty phenomenon in the section aptly named, OVERLOAD. First we need to locate your public school or schools.

Locating Your Public School

Contact your school district by either calling or logging onto their website to verify your public school. Refer to your target district's QUICK FACTS for contact information. Some districts assign kids to one specific neighborhood school based on home address. Other school districts assign schools by a combination of family preference and a lottery. A more detailed discussion of the lottery process is summarized in SCHOOL LOTTERIES.

 Before you buy or lease a residence verify what school district you will be located in from the school district. **Do not rely on a landlord, current owner, real estate agent or potential neighbors to provide this information.** School districts change their boundaries, new schools open, and schools have been known to close. In addition, your zip code or mailing address does not automatically confirm your assignment to a specific school district. Emeryville for example, has a 94608 zip code as do certain parts of Oakland. In some neighborhoods the school you are assigned to may be different from your neighbors across the street. It is imperative that you find out which school or school zone your child is eligible to attend directly from the school district.

How and When to Get Started

Contact your neighborhood school, school district or log onto their website to find out *specific* dates of registration for your target school(s). Familiarize yourself with the requirements your target school(s) and district(s) stipulate sooner as opposed to later. Ideally, start making calls and logging onto websites in the fall before your child will begin kindergarten. Many schools provide a kindergarten registration packet, complete with forms and instructions on how and when to register. If you have done your homework prior to this, re-contact your target school(s) to make sure their registration process, as well as school boundaries has not changed.

Families are required to register their child for kindergarten in person at their neighborhood school or district office. Staff will go over the forms to make sure they are correct and complete, and in most school districts, photocopy the documents they need for their files. Your child is then immediately registered for that school unless your child is overloaded, requesting a transfer, or in a district that assigns schools by a lottery. Learn more about this in the sections entitled SCHOOL LOTTERIES and SCHOOL AND DISTRICT TRANSFERS.

School Visits

Prior to registering your child in public school, I strongly recommend you and your mates visit your target school(s). Attend an open house, find out if you can sit in on a kindergarten class, attend one or more school events, and make an effort to talk with families and staff, particularly the kindergarten teachers and principal. Some public schools may resist your efforts to visit. I was unfortunate to have one staff person angrily state, "I do not have the time to give you a tour" followed by the phone being slammed down in my ear. I tell you this not to induce anxiety or knock public school, but to warn you that many public schools are understaffed and do not have the time or resources to offer tours.

Keep in mind, private schools require families to take a school tour, public schools do not. Private schools have staff dedicated to organizing school visits, answering questions about admissions, and marketing and advertising their school. The public schools do not operate in this fashion. Does this mean one type of school is better than the other? No. You and your mates need to find the school that is best for your child. To make the most of your school visits, refer to SCHOOL VISITS in the PRIVATE SCHOOL section, for a detailed discussion.

If your target public school does not provide tours do not despair, contact the Parent Teacher Associate (PTA) and try to hook up with a family that has a child enrolled at this school. Attend a school event (make sure it is open to the public), and take a walk by school grounds when it is in session. Do what you can to get a feel for the school. Visiting a public school may be a bit more labor intensive but the information you gain is invaluable. Some school districts designate dates and times when schools will conduct tours. Do not show up at a school expecting a tour, always call ahead and if possible, schedule an appointment.

Neighborhood Associations

In recent years, several public school neighborhood associations have cropped up. These grass roots organizations were started by local parents. Their intent is to rally families to enroll their children in their neighborhood school. The Piedmont Avenue Neighborhood Association (PANSA) states, *"We think that after paying our rents and mortgages, we should have a great school right here in the North*

Oakland flats". These groups collaborate with the PTA and school staff. They support their schools by organizing and conducting fund raisers, volunteering at the school and generating a sense of local community. Contact your school to find out if such a group exists in your neighborhood or consider starting one of your own.

Registration Paperwork

Following is a summary of the various documents and forms you will need to provide and complete to register your child for kindergarten. Many school district websites provide downloadable forms. Your neighborhood school and school district will also have hard copies of these forms (e.g., immunizations, and physical and oral health exams).

Proof of Residency

Proving your residency is *mandatory* in all public school districts. Each district has its own requirements and process for verification. **You must bring in the appropriate original documents** (e.g., mortgage or rental agreement papers, utility bills) within the time frame specified by your district. The district will not keep these documents but may make photocopies. Several school districts allow or encourage families to schedule an appointment to expedite this process. Refer to the QUICK FACTS for specifics on your school district. **If you do not have a permanent residence, your child is still eligible to register for kindergarten** (see TRANSIENT FAMILIES section). Contact your local school or district to learn more.

Proof of Age

Your child must be **five years old on or before December 2nd to be eligible for kindergarten in the public schools**. Families must provide documentation of their child's age, such as a birth certificate. If you do not have an original birth certificate, check with your school district to determine which documents are acceptable, (e.g., passport, I-94).

Immunizations (yellow card)

California state law requires that children must have up-to-date immunizations. However, according to the California Department of Education website (www.cde.ca.gov),

Children are exempt from immunization requirements when (1) their parents sign a statement at the school indicating that such immunization is contrary to their beliefs; or (2) the parents submit a statement from a physician indicating that immunization is not considered safe for the child. An exemption may be temporary or permanent and may be for specific or all vaccines." Contact your school or district to learn more.

Physical Health Exam

The state of California also requires a physical exam prior to enrollment. The California Department of Education website indicates,

State law also requires each child's family to provide, within 90 days of entrance into the first grade, a certificate documenting that the child has received a health checkup within the prior 18 months. Parents may waive the health checkup requirement because they do not want or are unable to obtain a health screening for their child. If the waiver indicates that the parents were unable to obtain such services, then the reasons must be included in the waiver. Law requires school districts to exclude any first grader up to five days if the child has neither a health examination certificate nor a parental waiver 90 days after entering the first grade. Some children may be eligible for a state-paid examination. Referrals to doctors and clinics are provided on request by the Child Health and Disability Prevention (CHDP) program coordinator of the local health department. Children through age 18 may receive a free checkup funded by CHDP if their families meet specific income guidelines. Most county health departments have a CHDP coordinator who can advise parents regarding eligibility.

To find out if you qualify for free or low cost health examinations in Alameda County, contact one or both of the following:

> Alameda County Public Health Department
> 1000 Broadway Suite 500
> Oakland, CA 94607
> Phone: (510)267-8000
> Fax: (510)267-3212
> www.acphd.org

> Alameda County Child Health & Disability
> Prevention Program
> 1000 San Leandro Blvd, 2nd Floor
> San Leandro, CA 94577
> Phone: (510)618-2070
> Fax: (510)618-2077

Oral Health Exam

California recently passed legislation that requires all incoming kindergarten students to have an oral health assessment (dental check-up). The law indicates that the exam must be performed by a licensed dentist or other licensed or registered dental health professional. If your child receives regular dental check ups you may just need to have your dentist fill out the appropriate paperwork. Each school district has its own rules about when this exam needs to occur (e.g., no more than 6 months before the start of kindergarten). Contact your school district to learn more.

Transient Families: Temporary or Uncertain Housing

The *McKinney-Vento Homeless Education Assistance Improvements Act* and California state law, indicate that children are guaranteed a public education if their housing is uncertain, they have a temporary address or no permanent address.   According to the Alameda County Office of Education, if your family has this type of living situation, you do not need to provide the following documents to register and enroll your child in public school:

9- Proof of residency

9- Immunization records or tuberculosis skin-test results

9- School records

9- Legal guardianship papers

To learn more, contact your school district or the Alameda County liaison for the homeless at:

> Director, Student Programs and Services
> Alameda County Office of Education
> 313 W. Winton Avenue
> Hayward, CA 94544
> (510)670-7747

School Lotteries

School districts use a lottery system to determine school assignment for various reasons. Some school districts assign all children to schools by a lottery (i.e., Albany and Berkeley). The goal of the all school lottery is to make each of the schools within the district more equitable while enhancing diversity. Districts also use a lottery when there are more applicants than space available. This type of lottery can occur in two situations, overload or transfers.

Overload (district residents only)

Overload occurs when a neighborhood school has more children eligible to attend a particular school than space available. A lottery is held to determine which students will be enrolled at the overloaded school and which students will be sent to another school within the district. Contact your school district to find out if your neighborhood school has a history of overloading and if so, *kindly* interrogate the district staff on how your child can best avoid being overloaded. If you are overloaded, immediately get your child's name on the waiting list(s) for your desired school(s). Stay in contact with whoever is handling school placement (e.g., school principal, district staff). Space may become available over the summer or after the school year starts. If you are still gung ho about a particular school that you were overloaded out of, consider trying to obtain space for the following year (i.e., first grade). Talk with school and district staff about your options.

Transfers

Lotteries are also conducted for students seeking either an intra or interdistrict transfer. If space is available at a particular school, transfer students are often accepted into that school. Priority is first given to those residing within the neighborhood, then the district and then outside the district. To learn more about intra and interdistrict transfers refer to the section below entitled, SCHOOL AND DISTRICT TRANSFERS.

How a school district determines priority influences how they conduct their lottery. Read on to learn more.

A Word or Two About Priority

Baking cookies for the principal or other such shenanigans will not get your child into the kindergarten of your choice. Each district has its own guidelines about how schools are assigned and who is given priority. Following is a brief description of some of the factors affecting a given family's priority in the kindergarten admissions process.

Neighborhood resident

If your school district assigns a particular school (i.e., neighborhood school) based on your home address then you will receive priority over those families living within that district but who are not assigned to this particular neighborhood school. This is also true for districts that assign schools within a particular zone. If you choose to enroll your child in one or more schools within your designated zone, you have priority over district residents who do not live within this zone. If these schools are overloaded, you will have priority but will not necessarily be enrolled at your neighborhood or zone school(s).

School district resident

If you live within a particular school district you will receive priority over those not living within that district. If you wish to enroll your child in a public school within your school district that is not your designated school (or schools if a zone) then you must contact the district and apply for an *intradistrict transfer*. Refer below to SCHOOL AND DISTRICT TRANSFERS.

Siblings

Priority is almost always given to families with a child already enrolled at a particular school.

Need

> If your child has a special need (e.g., requires certain facilities, classes), safety is an issue, or your neighborhood school is a program improvement school, your child may be given priority within a school district. See STANDARDIZED TESTING to learn more about program improvement schools.

Paperwork deadlines

> Families correctly completing and returning their paperwork within a school district's designated registration time frame are given priority over those families who do not.

The take home message here is that district residents will always receive priority over those not living within a particular school district. In addition, need, siblings enrolled at a particular school, and correct and complete paperwork filed during the registration window, all factor into these tricky registration and enrollment decisions. Next, let us discuss how to tackle the transfer process.

School and District Transfers

There are two types of transfers available to families in the California public school system, intradistrict and interdistrict transfers. You do not need to apply for a transfer if your child enrolls in a private school or is home schooled. *Each school district has different rules about if and how transfers are granted.* Please refer to the QUICK FACTS and contact your target school district(s) to learn more.

Intradistrict Transfer

> An intradistrict transfer is a request to transfer to a public school *within* your current school district. Some districts require families to reapply annually for an intradistrict transfer. Other districts designate this school as your family's new neighborhood

school until your child graduates from this particular school. Your family will need to register for middle and high school and school assignment will again be determined by either your home address or zone. If you desire a different middle or high school within your school district, your family will need to reapply for an intradistrict transfer. **Keep in mind, filling out the paperwork does not guarantee that your family will be granted an intradistrict transfer.** Finally, unless otherwise indicated, transportation to school is your family's responsibility.

Interdistrict Transfer

An interdistrict transfer is a request to transfer *out* of your public school district and into another public school district (e.g., from Pleasanton to Alameda). To obtain an interdistrict transfer, first contact your current public school district with your request. They will then have you complete the necessary forms. **Note, filling out the paperwork for an interdistrict transfer does not guarantee the transfer.** Three things must occur in order for you to successfully obtain an interdistrict transfer: release, acceptance and space.

- ✧ *Release* - Your current school district must "release" your child from the district. Families must justify on the interdistrict transfer application, why they desire the transfer (e.g., your child will be closer to where you work or after care arrangements). Some districts are more laid back about releasing potential students while others are not.

- ✧ *Acceptance* - The district you want to transfer into must be willing to accept your child. Some school districts are closed, that is they do not accept any interdistrict transfers. Others may be open but may not accept your child for other reasons (e.g., no space available, special needs district or school unable to accommodate, child's history of behavior problems). Contact the district you want to transfer into before filling out the paperwork.

✧ *Space* - The school or schools you want your child to attend must have space available. Residents will be placed first and once this is complete your child will be offered a spot if there is still room.

If your child is granted an interdistrict transfer, transportation to school is your family's responsibility. In addition, almost all of the Alameda County school districts require families to annually reapply for an interdistrict transfer. It is important to note that a given district's requirement to annually reapply for a transfer, does not necessarily mean it is impossible to attend a school via transfer. For the most part, districts will make the effort to retain your child unless there are extenuating circumstances (e.g., influx of district residents, boundary changes, school closures, behavior problems from your child). If your request for an interdistrict transfer is denied, you can first appeal to the school district. If you are denied at the district level, you can submit an appeal to the Alameda County Board of Education. An application and handbook detailing the appeal process is available from:

Alameda County Office of Education (ACOE)
313 W. Winton Avenue.
Hayward, CA 94544
(510)887-0152
www.acoe.k12.ca.us

Kindergarten Schedule

Kindergarteners have a shorter school day than their upper classmates. Some public schools offer families the choice of sending their children to kindergarten in morning or the afternoon. In addition, one day a week (typically Wednesday) schools have an early dismissal, referred to as a minimum day. Check with your school to learn about class schedules for each grade. In addition, a few schools within some of the districts offer a year round schedule.

Before & After Care

All of the school districts within Alameda County have arranged some form of extended care. Care is not necessarily offered onsite or by the district, most often it is contracted with a private company. In addition, not all of the schools within a district provide extended care. Check the QUICK FACTS to learn more about your district's childcare options.

Busing

Some of the school districts within Alameda County offer busing for a fee. Eligibility for each district varies. The state of California has also passed legislation that children with special needs are eligible for busing. Check with your school district to determine if your child is eligible.

English Language Learners & Language Testing

If your child's first language is not English, he will be given the California English Language Development Test (CELDT) in the beginning weeks of school. The CELDT assesses your child's English language proficiency. The CELDT is free, provided by the school and will help determine if and what language support your child will need. The CELDT is repeated every year until language support is no longer needed.

Standardized Tests

Standardized test scores are a fact of public school life. A particular school or district's test scores is another piece of data your family can use when deciding on a school. School and district websites often post their most recent test scores. The California Department of Education (www.cde.ca.gov) and Great Schools (www.greatschools.net)--a fantastic online resource—also provide test score information. These two websites also provide detailed descriptions of the tests and interpretations of the scores. Information can be broken down by district and individual school. Following is a brief description of terms to help familiarize you with California's standardized testing.

Standardized Testing and Reporting (STAR)
> The STAR is California's standardized testing program. All public school students in grades 2 through 11 are required to take a battery of standardized tests in mid to late spring.

Academic Performance Index (API)
> The API is a single score that incorporates each of the standardized test scores administered to students. API scores can range from 200 to 1000, with higher scores indicating better performance. The state has set a goal of 800 for all schools. The API is converted into a 1 to 10 score, where 1 is equal to the lowest performing schools and 10 is the highest performing schools.

Program Improvement (PI)
> A PI school is one that has not met certain benchmarks (test scores) consecutively for at least

two years. PI schools lose their PI status if they consistently raise their test scores to a certain level two years in a row. According to the California Department of Education website (www.cde.ca.gov),

> *[Program Improvement] schools are subject to a range of requirements and local interventions if they fail to meet improvement benchmarks under NCLB. For instance, all schools identified as being in PI must offer choice for their students to attend another school in the district that is not designated as being a PI school and must provide paid transportation.*

No Child Left Behind (NCLB)
The NCLB Act of 2001 is federal legislation that mandates educational reform in several key areas of education. For a detailed description of this act, go to the U. S. Department of Education website at www.ed.gov.

A Quick Note about Quick Facts

The following section is a summary of each public school district within Alameda County. These QUICK FACTS pages provide general information about each district's kindergarten admissions process. The information in these QUICK FACTS was obtained by interviewing district staff and downloading and reviewing district and individual school websites. Almost all districts were cooperative and forthcoming. Be advised that district, state and federal educational policy is a moving target and therefore can change quickly. Many districts periodically tweak their registration process, often trying to accommodate new governmental mandates or a fluctuating population (think: overload or school closures). It is worth repeating, that the QUICK FACTS are intended to serve as a starting place for you and your search mates. **Contact your target school(s) and**

school district(s) to obtain specific dates, deadlines, as well as changes in policy and procedure. Once you have had a look, we will wrap up our discussion about final school decision making in CHOOSING A SCHOOL.

School District Quick Facts: Alameda County

Alameda

Alameda Unified School District (AUSD)
2200 Central Avenue
Alameda, CA 94501
(510)337-7060 main
(510)337-7072 student services
www.alameda.k12.ca.us

Elementary School Facts

Schools

* 10 elementary schools:
    * 9 schools are Kindergarten through 5th grade.
    * 1 school (Bay Farm) is Kindergarten through 6th grade.
* Placement is determined by home address.

Kindergarten Schedule

* ~8:00 AM to 12:45 PM/1:45 PM
* Kindergarteners are placed in one of two groups, these groups alternate between early (12:45 PM) and late (1:45 PM) dismissal times twice a week.

School Visits

* *Kindergarten Information Night* typically offered in January on the same date by each elementary school.
* Tours are typically offered in January and February, contact schools directly to set up a tour.

Before & After Care

* Onsite care: Island Kids (510)769-8545
* Offsite care: Kindercare (510)521-3227 and Garner Learning (510)769-5437

Busing
* Special needs students only.

Registration & Enrollment

Dates & Deadlines
* Registration packets available in January.

* 🦌 **Correctly complete and return registration documents as soon as possible since** *placement is based on a first come first serve basis* (see *Process & Procedures*)

* School offices close in the summer and re-open two weeks before the new school year starts.

Process & Procedures
* Registration takes place onsite at the elementary school on a first come first serve basis.

* 🦌 *Overload* is an issue at some elementary schools.

* 🦌 **Because of the first come first serve method of registration, at some schools, parents have begun standing in line hours, often the night before registration begins (in January), to secure a space.** Contact your target school(s) to determine when registration will begin and ask staff if overload is an issue so that you can make a game plan if standing in line is a necessity.

Documents ****Bring original documents****
* 3 proofs of residency required, acceptable documents include:
  ↳ Rental agreement, mortgage papers or property tax bill.

  ↳ Two utility bills (Alameda Power & Telecom, garbage, water).

* Picture ID of parent or legal guardian.

* Proof of Age (e.g., birth certificate).

* Proof of Immunizations (yellow card).

* Proof of Health Exam form completed by physician or medical professional.

* Proof of Oral Health Exam form completed by dentist.

Transfers

Intradistrict—Alameda Residents Only
* Contact the AUSD offices and request an intradistrict transfer. If space is available, students will be put on a waiting list.

* Waiting lists begin in May.

Interdistrict
* <u>Alameda Residents</u> – Contact the AUSD to obtain an interdistrict transfer form.

* <u>Non-Alameda Residents</u> – Contact your current school district to obtain an interdistrict transfer form. Once Alameda residents are placed your child will then be offered a spot if there is space available.

Albany

Albany Unified School District (AlbUSD)
904 Talbot Avenue
Albany, CA 94706
(510)558-3750
www.albany.k12.ca.us

Elementary School Facts

Schools
* 3 elementary schools are Kindergarten through 5th grade.
* Placement is determined by lottery.
* Families have 6 options to choose from [3 schools x 2 times (i.e., morning or afternoon)].

Kindergarten Schedule
* Morning ~8:00 AM to 11:30 AM
* Afternoon ~11:50 AM to 3:10 PM

School Visits
* Tours offered Tuesday mornings when school is in session, contact school(s) to make an appointment.

Before & After Care
* Extended care is available at all of the elementary schools. The AlbUSD has contracts with private companies for both onsite and offsite care. Contact each of the schools to learn more.

Busing
* Special needs students only.

Registration & Enrollment

Dates & Deadlines
- ✳ Contact the AlbUSD and make an appointment to verify your residency.

- ✳ Registration packets are mailed in March to families who verify their residency in February. Priority is given to these families.

- ✳ Completed forms need to be returned in April.

- ✳ School assignments are mailed in the summer.

- ✳ If you begin the process later than February, check with the district office on deadlines and notifications.

Process & Procedures
- ✳ Registration occurs at the district office.

- ✳ AlbUSD tries to honor your school choices however preference is given to those families who return their enrollment forms by the deadline and have older siblings already enrolled at a particular school.

Documents **Bring original documents****
- ✳ 3 proofs of residency required, acceptable documents include:
  - ↪ Rental agreement, mortgage or property tax bill.
  - ↪ Utility bill, public assistance or payroll documents.

- ✳ Picture ID of parent or legal guardian.

- ✳ Proof of Age (e.g., birth certificate).

- ✳ Proof of Immunizations (yellow card).

* Proof of Health Exam form completed by physician or medical professional.

* Proof of Oral Health Exam form completed by dentist.

* Starting in February, parents can bring documents to the district office for verification – call ahead for an appointment.

Transfers

Intradistrict—Albany Residents Only
* Write a letter addressed to the principals of the schools involved (i.e., school you want to transfer into and school you want to transfer out of) requesting a transfer. Your child's name will then be put on a waiting list.

Interdistrict
* <u>Albany Residents</u> – Contact the AlbUSD to obtain an interdistrict transfer form.

* <u>Non-Albany Residents</u> – ***Closed*** Interdistrict transfers are only available to those parents who work for the school district.

Berkeley

Berkeley Unified School District (BUSD)
Admissions & Attendance Office
1835 Allston Way
Berkeley, CA 94704
(510)644-6504
www.berkeley.k12.ca.us

Elementary School Facts

Schools

* 11 elementary schools are Kindergarten through 5th grade.

* BUSD is divided into 3 zones: Northwest, Central & Southeast (3-4 schools per zone); log onto the BUSD website or contact their office to determine your zone.

* Placement is determined by lottery within 3 school zones (see *Process & Procedures* below).

Kindergarten Schedule

* Depending on the school, ~8:00 AM to 1:30 PM or ~9:00 AM to 2:30 PM.

School Visits

* *Informational School Fair* - Representatives from all BUSD schools answer questions and provide information about their schools. Typically held in December or January.

* *Informational School Nights* - Offered at each elementary school in January. These events differ from the Informational School Fair since they are held onsite and focus on individual school programs.

* Tours offered on Tuesday and Thursday mornings November through early February. Contact schools to set up an appointment.

Before & After Care
* Before school care is offered at seven of the elementary schools and aftercare is offered at all Berkeley public schools.

* Sliding scale fees available.

Busing
* Free transportation is available to those students living more than 1 mile from their school and that school is within their designated school zone.

* Those attending school on an intradistrict transfer are not eligible for busing since their school is outside of their designated school zone.

Registration & Enrollment

Dates & Deadlines
* Registration packets are available in December and due in February to receive priority.

* Decisions on school placement are mailed in March.

Process & Procedures
* Registration takes place at the BUSD, download the *Parent Preference Form* from the BUSD website or pick up a hard copy directly from the BUSD.

* Families can request any school within the BUSD however priority is given to families residing within a particular zone.

Documents ****Bring original documents****

* 3 proofs of residency required (*at least one document must be a current utility bill*), acceptable documents include:
  ↳ PG& E bill

  ↳ EBMUD bill

  ↳ Telephone bill (non-celluar)

  ↳ Cable or waste management bill

  ↳ Bank statement

* Picture ID of parent or legal guardian.

* Proof of Age (e.g., birth certificate).

* Proof of Immunizations (yellow card).

* Proof of Health Exam form completed by physician or medical professional.

* Proof of Oral Health Exam form completed by dentist.

Transfers

Intradistrict—Berkeley Residents Only

* Write a letter addressed to the principals of each schools involved (i.e., school transferring into and school transferring out of) requesting a transfer. Your child's name will be put on a waiting list.

Interdistrict

* <u>Berkeley Residents</u> – Contact the BUSD to obtain an interdistrict transfer form.

* <u>Non-Berkeley Residents</u> – Contact your current school district to obtain an interdistrict transfer form.   Once Berkeley residents are placed (shortly after school begins) your child will then be offered a spot if space is available.

Castro Valley

Castro Valley Unified School District (CVUSD)
4400 Alma Avenue
Castro Valley, CA 94546
(510)537-3000
www.cv.k12.ca.us

Elementary School Facts

Schools

* 9 elementary schools are Kindergarten through 5th grade.

* Placement is determined by home address.

Kindergarten Schedule

* ~8:00 AM to Noon/1:00 PM or ~11:30/Noon to 3:00/3:30 PM.

* Kindergarten schedules vary across all of the CVUSD schools. Check with your school to learn more out specific times.

School Visits

* Contact individual schools to set up a tour or learn more about open house events.

Before & After Care

* Onsite extended care is available at all of the elementary schools except Palomares Elementary.

Busing

* Special needs students only at the elementary school level.

* Busing is available to middle and high school students.

Registration & Enrollment

Dates & Deadlines
* Registration begins in March.

* Lotteries are conducted in April or May.

Process & Procedures

* *Overload* is an issue at some of the elementary schools.

* A lottery will be conducted if overload occurs. Ask to be put on a waiting list if your child is overloaded.

Documents ****Bring original documents****
* 3 proofs of residency required, acceptable documents include:
    ↪ Rental agreement, county tax bill or signed and dated escrow documents.

    ↪ PG & E bill

    ↪ One other bill or document - EBMUD, telephone, credit card, hospital, or physician's bill, preprinted DMV California ID or driver's license.

* Home owner's or renter's statement of residency.

* Picture ID of parent or legal guardian.

* Proof of Age (e.g., birth certificate).

* Proof of Immunizations (yellow card).

* Proof of Health Exam form completed by physician or medical professional.

* Proof of Oral Health Exam form completed by dentist.

Transfers

Intradistrict—Castro Valley Residents Only

* Contact the CVUSD offices and request an intradistrict transfer. If space is available, students will be put on a waiting list.

* Intradistrict transfer decisions are made by the principals.

* Kindergarten through 5th grade intradistrict requests have been accepted throughout April.

* Families must reapply every year.

Interdistrict

* Castro Valley Residents – Contact the CVUSD to obtain an interdistrict transfer form.

* Non-Castro Valley Residents – Contact your current school district to obtain an interdistrict transfer form. Once Castro Valley residents are placed your child will then be offered a spot if there is space available. Families must reapply annually.

Dublin

Dublin Unified School District (DUSD)
7471 Larkdale Avenue
Dublin, CA 94568
(925)828-2551
www.dublin.k12.ca.us

Elementary School Facts

Schools
- ✳ 7 elementary schools:
  - ↪ 5 schools are Kindergarten through 5th grade.
  - ↪ 1 new school (Green Elementary) is Kindergarten through 4th grade for 2007-2008; in subsequent years it will be Kindergarten through 5th grade.
  - ↪ 1 school (Fallon) is Kindergarten through 8th grade.
  - ↪ The DUSD offers a multi-age K-3rd parent participation program called *Pathways*. This alternative program is offered at Murray Elementary School and is open to all K-3 students enrolled in DUSD.
- ✳ Placement is determined by home address.
- ✳ 🦌 Due to the opening of Green Elementary, **school district zones have changed**. Contact the DUSD to determine which elementary school your child is eligible to attend.

Kindergarten Schedule
- ✳ ~8:30 AM to Noon

School Visits
* Contact individual schools to set up a tour or learn more about open house events.

Before & After Care
All DUSD elementary schools provide before and after care. Contact the following organizations for more information:

* Extended Day Child Care: (925)803-4154

* City of Dublin After School Recreation on campus: (925)556-4500

* Child Care Links (Non Profit Child Care referral program): (925)417-8733

Busing
* Special needs students only.

Registration & Enrollment

Dates & Deadlines
* Registration packets are available on the first day of registration in March.

Process & Procedures
* Registration takes place onsite at your neighborhood school.

Documents **Bring original documents**
* 2 proofs of residency required, acceptable documents include:
  ↳ Rental agreement or mortgage papers.
  ↳ Utility or insurance bill (PG&E, DSRSD, homeowner's insurance).

* Picture ID of parent or legal guardian.

* Proof of Age (e.g., birth certificate).

* Proof of Immunizations (yellow card).

* Proof of Health Exam form completed by physician or medical professional.

* Proof of Oral Health Exam form completed by dentist.

* Your child's Social Security Number.

Transfers

Intradistrict—Dublin Residents Only
* Contact the DUSD offices and request an intradistrict transfer. Forms can be downloaded from the DUSB website or are available at all of the schools in February.

* Applications are due in April and accepted through the last day of school. Families are notified in May.

* Requests made after the last day of school will not be considered until the second week of school in September.

* A lottery will be conducted if requests exceed space available.

* Families *do not* need to reapply annually for an intradistrict transfer.

Interdistrict
* Dublin Residents – Contact the DUSD to obtain an interdistrict transfer form.

* Non-Dublin Residents – Contact your current school district to obtain an interdistrict transfer form. Once Dublin residents are placed your child will then be offered a spot if there is space available. Families must reapply annually. Renewal applications have been accepted starting in April.

Emeryville

Emeryville Unified School District (EUSD)
4727 San Pablo Avenue
Emeryville, CA 94608
(510)601-4000
www.emeryusd.k12.ca.us

Elementary School Facts

Schools
* 1 elementary school, Kindergarten through 6th grade.
* Placement is determined by home address.

Kindergarten Schedule
* ~8:30 AM to 1:30 PM

School Visits
* Open house in January or February.
* Tuesday morning tours when school is in session, call the district office to schedule an appointment.

Before & After Care
* Before and after care offered by the Emeryville Recreation Department (510)596-4395.
* Children are walked to and from school daily.

Busing
* Special needs students only.

Registration & Enrollment

Dates & Deadlines
* Registration packets available year round.
* Enrollment begins "in earnest" in February.

Process & Procedures
* Registration takes place at the district office.

* At the time of this printing, *Overload* was not a concern.

Documents ****Bring original documents****
* 2 proofs of residency required, acceptable documents include:
    ↳ Rental agreement or mortgage papers.

    ↳ Utility bills (e.g., PG&E, garbage, phone, cable).

* Picture ID of parent or legal guardian.

* Proof of Age (e.g., birth certificate).

* Proof of Immunizations (yellow card).

* Proof of Health Exam form completed by physician or medical professional.

* Proof of Oral Health Exam form completed by dentist.

Transfers

Intradistrict—Emeryville Residents Only
* Since there is only one elementary school, there are no intradistrict transfers.

Interdistrict
* Emeryville Residents – Contact the EUSD to obtain an interdistrict transfer form.

* Non-Emeryville Residents – Contact your current school district to obtain an interdistrict transfer form. Once Emeryville residents are placed your child will then be offered a spot if space is available. Families must reapply annually.

Fremont

Fremont Unified School District (FUSD)
4210 Technology Drive
Fremont, CA 94538
(510)657-2350 – Main
(510)659-2534 – Pupil Services
www.fremont.k12.ca.us

Elementary School Facts

Schools
- 29 elementary schools:
  - 27 schools are Kindergarten through 6th grade.
  - 1 school (James Leitch) is Kindergarten through 2nd grade.
  - 1 school (Warm Springs) is 3rd through 6th grade.
- Placement is determined by home address.

Kindergarten Schedule
- Kindergarten schedules vary across schools. Some schools offer morning and afternoon schedules while others offer early morning and later morning classes.
- A typical kindergarten day is approximately 3.5 hours long.

School Visits
- Open house offered in the spring at most schools.
- Contact individual schools to learn more about school visits and kindergarten orientation.

Before & After Care
* Extended care offered at *some* FUSD schools by:
  ↳ Fremont-Newark YMCA (510)657-5200
  ↳ Adventure Time (510)658-3516
  ↳ Bay Area Child Care at (510)490-4222

Busing
* Busing, for a fee, is available to elementary students living more than 1 mile from school. Contact the district transportation office at: (510) 657-1450.
* Free and reduced rate bus passes are available for households that meet income eligibility guidelines.
* AC Transit buses also serve many of FUSB's school sites.

Registration & Enrollment

Dates & Deadlines
* Registration packets available in February.
* Priority given to families who correctly complete and return their documents by March deadline.

Process & Procedures
* Registration takes place onsite at the elementary school.
* 🦌 *Overload* is an issue at some elementary schools.
* For those overloaded, a lottery will be held in March to determine school placement.
* If overloaded to another school and space becomes available **before January 31**, families

have the option of returning to their neighborhood school.

* 🦌 According to the FUSD website,
You should register your school age student as soon as you are a Fremont resident to establish your eligibility to attend the attendance area school. The earlier you register, the greater chance your child will have in the choice of courses at the secondary level and space availability at the elementary level. Only official registration will place your child in the school registration book and hold a space for your child at that school.

Documents ****Bring original documents****

* 4 proofs of residency required, acceptable documents include:
  ↳ Rental agreement or mortgage payment

  ↳ PG & E bill

  ↳ Other utility bill (water, telephone)

  ↳ One other bill mailed to your residence (cable, garbage, credit card, hospital or physician)

* Picture ID of parent or legal guardian.

* Proof of Age (e.g., birth certificate).

* Proof of Immunizations (yellow card).

* Proof of Health Exam form completed by physician or medical professional.

* Proof of Oral Health Exam form completed by dentist.

Transfers

Intradistrict—Fremont Residents Only

*   ✳ Contact Pupil Services at: (510)659-2534 to request an application for an intradistrict transfer. If space is available, students will be put on a waiting list.

*   ✳ Families must reapply annually.

Interdistrict

*   ✳ <u>Fremont Residents</u> – Contact the FUSD to obtain an interdistrict transfer form.

*   ✳ <u>Non-Fremont Residents</u> – Contact your current school district to obtain an interdistrict transfer form. Once Fremont residents are placed your child will then be offered a spot if space is available. Families must reapply annually.

Hayward

Hayward Unified School District (HUSD)
24411 Amador Street
Hayward, CA 94540
(510)784-2600
www.husd.k12.ca.us

Elementary School Facts

Schools

* 25 elementary schools:
  * 18 schools are Kindergarten through 6th grade.
  * 3 schools are Kindergarten through 3rd grade (Glassbrook, Ruus, Shephard).
  * 1 school is Kindergarten through 1st grade (Treeview-Bidwell).
  * 1 school is 2nd through 6th (Treeview).
  * 2 schools are 4th through 6th grade (Ruus Peixoto, Tyrrell).

* Placement is determined by home address.

* **3 or 4 schools are closing for 2007-2008 school year** (see *Process & Procedures* below).

Kindergarten Schedule

* Kindergarten schedules vary across schools. Some schools offer both morning and afternoon schedules while others offer early morning and later morning classes.

* A typical kindergarten day is approximately 3.5 hours long.

* 4 elementary schools (Bowman, East Avenue, Eldridge, Park) follow a year round schedule.

School Visits
 * Contact schools directly to set up a school visit.

Before & After Care
 * Latchkey Program (510)783-5437 - Year round extended care is offered at all HUSD elementary schools.

 * Youth Enrichment Program (YEP) (510)784-2600 x2778 – After care and summer programs offered to all HUSD elementary and middle school students. Sponsored by the city of Hayward Recreation and Park District.

Busing
 * Busing is offered by the HUSD. To determine eligibility and enroll, contact the transportation offices at: (510)784-2673.

Registration & Enrollment

Dates & Deadlines
 * Registration packets are available in March.

Process & Procedures
 * Registration takes place onsite at the elementary schools.

 * School district *boundary lines have been re-drawn* for the 2007-2008 school year. It is unclear if 3 or 4 schools will be closing (see below). Unfortunately, repeated calls to the HUSD has resulted in no confirmation of this information. The following statement was taken directly from the HUSD website:

 In [an] effort to balance school enrollments and remain fiscally solvent, the Board of Education has adopted an optimal school size and approved the closure of four schools and the consolidation of two schools. As a result, Hayward Unified School District is in the process of redrawing the attendance boundaries at all school levels. The new boundaries will be in effect for the 2007-08 school year, however the majority of students will remain at their current school. Only new enrollees, including kindergartners, 7th and 9th graders will be assigned to their new attendance boundaries.

All new students, including kindergartners, 7th and 9th graders will be assigned to the new school attendance boundaries. Schools slated for closure (Glassbrook, Markham and Muir) will have no kindergarten class in Fall 2007. http://www.husd.k12.ca.us/PDF/Boundary/HUSD% 20Boundaries%20Brochure.pdf

Documents ****Bring original documents****

* 2 proofs of residency required, acceptable documents include:
  ↳ Rental agreement, mortgage papers or property tax bill.
  ↳ Utility bills (PG&E, telephone, cable, garbage, water).
* Picture ID of parent or legal guardian.
* Proof of Age (e.g., birth certificate).
* Proof of Immunizations (yellow card).
* Proof of Health Exam form completed by physician or medical professional.
* Proof of Oral Health Exam form completed by dentist.

Transfers

Intradistrict—Hayward Residents Only
* Contact the HUSD offices and request an intradistrict transfer, referred to as *Open Enrollment*.

* Open Enrollment applications are available in early March and due by the end of March.

* Applications must be turned into your current neighborhood school or the HUSD's Child Welfare and Attendance office.

* A lottery will be conducted if there are more requests than space available.

Interdistrict
* Hayward Residents – Contact the HUSD to obtain an interdistrict transfer form. Forms are available in April.

* Non-Hayward Residents – Contact your current school district to obtain an interdistrict transfer form. You are also required to complete an application form from the HUSD. To receive priority complete and return your application during open enrollment in March. Once Hayward residents are placed your child will then be offered a spot if there is space available.

Livermore

Livermore Valley Joint Unified School District (LVJUSD)
685 East Jack London Boulevard
Livermore, CA 94551
(925)606-3200
www.livermoreschools.com

Elementary School Facts

Schools
- 11 elementary schools:
  - 10 schools are Kindergarten through 5th grade.
  - 1 school (Vineyard Elementary) 1st through 12th grade – Vineyard is for home schooled children. Contact the LVJUSD to learn more.
- Placement is determined by home address, however all eligible Livermore residents can attend Vineyard Elementary.

Kindergarten Schedule
- Morning ~8:00 AM to 11:30 AM
- Afternoon ~11:40 AM to 3:00 PM
- Not all of the elementary schools offer morning and afternoon kindergarten.

School Visits
- Each school sponsors an open house, typically in March or April in the evening.
- Contact individual schools to set up a tour.

Before & After Care
- ✳ Livermore Area Park & Recreation Department (925)373-5780 offers on site extended care at all 10 elementary schools.

Busing
- ✳ Special needs students only.

Registration & Enrollment

Dates & Deadlines
- ✳ Registration, also known as Open Enrollment begins in March.
- ✳ Correctly complete and return packet documents during the specified Open Enrollment dates to receive priority.

Process & Procedures
- ✳ Registration takes place onsite at the elementary school, open enrollment dates and times vary among the schools. Contact your neighborhood school directly to set up an appointment.
- ✳ Walk in registration takes place onsite, after the Open Enrollment period.

Documents ****Bring original documents****
- ✳ 2 proofs of residency are required, acceptable documents include:
  - ↳ Rental agreement or escrow papers;

    OR
  - ↳ Utility bill (PG&E, water, cable, garbage).
- ✳ Picture ID of parent or legal guardian.
- ✳ Proof of Age (e.g., birth certificate).
- ✳ Proof of Immunizations (yellow card).

* Proof of Health Exam form completed by physician or medical professional.

* Proof of Oral Health Exam form completed by dentist.

* Emergency contact information.

* Child's social security number (optional).

Transfers

Intradistrict — Livermore Residents Only
* Contact the LVJUSD and request an intradistrict transfer.

* A lottery is conducted after the Open Enrollment period if there are more requests than space available.

* Families will be notified by the end of the school year.

* Families do not need to reapply annually.

Interdistrict

* <u>Livermore Residents</u> – Contact the LVJUSD to obtain an interdistrict transfer form.

* <u>Non-Livermore Residents</u> – Contact your current school district to obtain an interdistrict transfer form. Once Livermore residents are placed your child will then be offered a spot if there is space available. A lottery is conducted if there are more requests than space available. Students are initially placed after the first few days of school. Families must reapply annually.

Mountain House

Mountain House School District (MHSD)
3950 Mountain House Road
Byron, CA 94514
(209)835-2283
www.mountainhouseschool.com

Elementary School Facts

Schools
* 1 multi-graded elementary school that is Kindergarten through 8th grade.

* Placement is determined by home address.

* According to MHSD website, *"There is only one school in this unique small district and the building that houses that school has been there for over 100 years."*

* 🦌 Mountain House School is located in a rural community in Eastern Alameda County. This school/school district **should not be confused with the Byron Unified School District** located in Contra Costa County, and located in the city of Byron.

Kindergarten Schedule
* ~8:20 AM to 12:10 PM

School Visits
* Contact the Mountain House School to set up a tour.

* A Back to School Night is offered to parents in September.

Before & After Care
* MHSD offers on site extended care.

Busing
* A new air conditioned bus is available to pick up students.

Registration & Enrollment

Dates & Deadlines
* Registration is relatively informal and can be conducted any time throughout the school year.

Process & Procedures
* Registration takes place at the Mountain House School.

Documents **Bring original documents****
* 1 proof of residency required, a current telephone or utility bill is acceptable.

* Picture ID of parent or legal guardian.

* Proof of Age (e.g., birth certificate).

* Proof of Immunizations (yellow card).

* Proof of Health Exam form completed by physician or medical professional.

* Proof of Oral Health Exam form completed by dentist.

Transfers

Intradistrict—MHSD Residents Only
* Since there is only one elementary school, there are no intradistrict transfers.

Interdistrict
* <u>MHSD Residents</u> – Contact the MHSD to obtain an interdistrict transfer form.

✳ <u>Non-MHSD Residents</u> – Contact your current school district to obtain an interdistrict transfer form. Once MHSD residents are placed your child will then be offered a spot if there is space available.

Newark

Newark Unified School District (NUSD)
5715 Musick Avenue
Newark, CA 94560
(510)818-4112
www.nusd.k12.ca.us

Elementary School Facts

Schools
* 8 elementary schools are Kindergarten through 6th grade.
* Placement is determined by home address.

Kindergarten Schedule
* ~8:00 AM to Noon

School Visits
* Site based kindergarten orientation available to registered families.
* Contact individual schools to set up a tour.

Before & After Care
* On site before and after care available at four elementary schools (Bunker, Kennedy, Musick, and Snow Child).
* On site after care offered at two schools (Lincoln and Milani).
* Contact the NUSD (510-818-4138) to learn more.

Busing
* Special needs students only.

Registration & Enrollment

Dates & Deadlines
* Registration begins in March.

* Priority given to families who correctly complete and return packet documents during the specified enrollment period.

Process & Procedures
* Registration takes place onsite at the elementary school, enrollment dates and times vary among the schools.

* Contact your neighborhood school directly to set up an appointment.

* *Overload* is an issue at some NUSD schools.

Documents **Bring original documents**
* 2 proofs of residency are required, acceptable documents include:
    ↪ Rental agreement or mortgage statement.

    ↪ Current PG&E bill.

* Picture ID of parent or legal guardian.

* Proof of Age (e.g., birth certificate).

* Proof of Immunizations (yellow card).

* Proof of Health Exam form completed by physician or medical professional.

* Proof of Oral Health Exam form completed by dentist.

Transfers

Intradistrict—Newark Residents Only
* Contact the NUSD and request an intradistrict transfer.

* A lottery is conducted if there are more requests for a particular school, then space available.

* Families are notified at the end of August.

* Families *do not need to reapply* annually for an intradistrict transfer.

Interdistrict

* Newark Residents – Contact the NUSD to obtain an interdistrict transfer form.

* Non-Newark Residents – Contact your current school district to obtain an interdistrict transfer form. Once Newark residents are placed your child will then be offered a spot if there is space available. A lottery is conducted if there are more requests than space available. Families must reapply annually.

Oakland

Oakland Unified School District (OUSD)
Student Assignment Office
1098 2nd Avenue, Portable 18
Oakland, CA 94606
(510)879-8111
www.ousd.k12.ca.us

Elementary School Facts

Schools
* 75 elementary schools, 11 of these schools are charter schools.

* Placement is determined by home address, however all eligible Oakland residents can apply to attend any school within the district by participating in the *Options Fair* (see description below).

Kindergarten Schedule
* ~8:30 AM to 2:45 PM

School Visits
* *Options Fair* is held in early January. Representatives from all of the schools within the OUSD are available to answer questions and provide information.

* Contact individual schools to set up a tour.

Before & After Care
* There are many different after school programs offered throughout the OUSD. Contact your neighborhood school to learn more.

Busing
* Special needs students only.

Registration & Enrollment

Dates & Deadlines
* Options forms are due by the specified deadline in January to receive priority.

* School placement decisions are mailed in March.

Process & Procedures
* Options forms are available online, at the OUSD offices, or any OUSD school.

* All families must complete an Options form, even if applying to your one neighborhood school.

* Families may choose up to 6 elementary schools within the OUSD.

* *Overload is an issue* at some of the elementary schools, therefore it is in your best interest to list more than 1 elementary school on your Options form.

* Options forms **must be submitted in person** at the Student Assignment Office (1098 2nd Ave, Oakland – Portable 18), or any OUSD elementary school.

* If there are more requests for a particular school than space available, a lottery will be conducted.

*Documents **Bring original documents***
* 3 proofs of residency required, acceptable documents include:
    ↳ Driver's license or official California ID Card from the Department of Motor Vehicles

    AND

    ↳ Home owner's or renter's insurance policy.

↪ Property tax statement.

↪ Current (within 90 days) utility bill (PG&E, home telephone, water, garbage, or cable).

↪ Automobile registration AND insurance (these documents count for two of the three required documents, **but must be provided together**).

↪ Official letter from a social services or government agency within 90 days.

* **Transitional families only**: If you do not have a permanent address (e.g., motel/hotel, shelter, car, or are living with relatives or friends) contact the Transitional Students and Families Program in Portable 15 at 1025 2nd Avenue in Oakland, for residency verification and assistance.

* Proof of Age (e.g., birth certificate).

* Proof of Immunizations (yellow card).

* Proof of Health Exam form completed by physician or medical professional.

* Proof of Oral Health Exam form completed by dentist.

Transfers

Intradistrict—Oakland Residents Only

* The OUSD is unique in that the intradistrict transfer process is the same as registering and enrolling in your neighborhood school. To request an intradistrict transfer, follow the same process and procedures outlined above in the section, *Process & Procedures*. **The same deadlines and rules apply**.

* 🦌 **You must register on time at your newly assigned school to retain your placement.** Contact your newly assigned school directly to find out when they are open for registration.

* Once placed, *families do not need to reapply* for an intradistrict transfer.

Interdistrict

* Oakland Residents – Contact the OUSD to obtain an interdistrict transfer form.

* Non-Oakland Residents – Contact your current school district to obtain an interdistrict transfer form. Once Oakland residents are placed your child will then be offered a spot if there is space available. Families must reapply annually.

Piedmont

Piedmont Unified School District (PUSD)
760 Magnolia Avenue
Piedmont, CA 94611
(510)594-2600
www.piedmont.k12.ca.us

Elementary School Facts

Schools
* 3 elementary schools – Kindergarten through 5th grade.

* Placement is determined by home address.

Kindergarten Schedule
* ~8:30 AM to Noon or ~10:30 AM to 2:00 PM

School Visits
* Contact individual schools to set up a tour.

Before & After Care
* School Mates (510)420-3078 offered by the Piedmont Recreation Department.

* All 3 elementary schools offer after school enrichment classes.

Busing
* Special needs students only.

Registration & Enrollment

Dates & Deadlines
* Registration begins in March.

* Correctly complete and return registration documents before specified deadline in March to receive priority.

Process & Procedures

* Registration takes place onsite at the elementary school in March.

* 🖐 *Overload occasionally occurs* among PUSD schools.

Documents ****Bring original documents****

* 4 proofs of residency are required, acceptable documents include:
  ↳ Grant deed *or* rental/lease contract,

    AND

  ↳ 3 additional documents such as: driver's license, credit card bill, bank account statement, insurance statement or utility bill.

* Picture ID of parent or legal guardian.

* Proof of Age (e.g., birth certificate).

* Proof of Immunizations (yellow card).

* Proof of Health Exam form completed by physician or medical professional.

* Proof of Oral Health Exam form completed by dentist.

Transfers

Intradistrict—Piedmont Residents Only

* Contact the PUSD offices and request an intradistrict transfer.

* A lottery is conducted if there are more requests for a particular school then school availability.

* School principals determine if transfers within the school district can or cannot be made.

Interdistrict

* <u>Piedmont Residents</u> – Contact the PUSD to obtain an interdistrict transfer form.

* <u>Non-Piedmont Residents</u> – ****Closed**** Interdistrict transfers are only available to those parents or legal guardians who work for the school district or the city of Piedmont *if space is available.*

Pleasanton

Pleasanton Unified School District (PLUSD)
4665 Bernal Avenue
Pleasanton, CA 94566-7498
(925)462-5500
www.pleasanton.k12.ca.us

Elementary School Facts

Schools
* 9 elementary schools are Kindergarten through 5th grade.
* Placement is determined by home address.

Kindergarten Schedule
* Morning ~8:00 AM to 11:30 AM
* Afternoon ~11:30 AM to 3:00 PM

School Visits
* *Kindergarten Information Night* held on multiple dates in February and March, includes a discussion of how to register and what to expect in kindergarten.
* *Kindergarten Back to School Night* has been held a few days before the school year begins.
* Contact individual schools to set up a tour.

Before & After Care
Extended care is available at all of PLUSD elementary schools. According to the district website the following programs are offered at the sites listed below:
* Kids Club (925)462-7625 – main number
  ↳ Alisal: (925)426-9751
  ↳ Donlon: (925)462-7083

- ↳ Hearst: (925)417-6602

- ↳ Valley View: (925)462-8805

- ↳ Vintage Hills: (925)484-4856

* Y-Kids
  - ↳ Fairlands: (925)426-1992

  - ↳ Lydiksen: (925)426-9784

  - ↳ Mohr: (925)484-9429

* EDCC
  - ↳ Walnut Grove School (925)846-5519

* Child Care Links at (925)417-8733 also provides a list of additional local child care options.

Busing
  * Special needs students only.

  * PLUSD and the City of Pleasanton sponsor RIDES to School, a program that matches up those wanting to carpool, bike, and/or walk to school together. To learn more, go to *www.pleasantonschoolpool.org*.

Registration & Enrollment

Dates & Deadlines
  * Kindergarten registration, also known as *Kindergarten Round-Up* takes place over 2 days in March.

Process & Procedures
  * *Kindergarten Round-Up* takes place in the Amador Valley High School Gym.

  * If you miss the *Kindergarten Round-Up*, you can register at your resident school site.

* ✋ *Overload is an issue at some of the elementary schools.*

Documents ****Bring original documents****
* 2 proofs of residency are required, acceptable documents include:
  ↳ Recent close of escrow papers, or recently signed rental/lease agreement.

  ↳ Current utility bill (such as PG&E, telephone, water, garbage, or cable TV).

  ↳ Note: If registration pre-dates the start of school attendance by more than a month, a second utility bill may be requested after the first month of student attendance.

* Picture ID of parent or legal guardian.

* Proof of Age (e.g., birth certificate).

* Proof of Immunizations (yellow card).

* Proof of Health Exam form completed by physician or medical professional.

* Proof of Oral Health Exam form completed by dentist.

* Child's social security number (*optional*).

* Parents' or legal guardian's employment information (for emergency contact).

Transfers

Intradistrict—Pleasanton Residents Only
* Applications are available from the PLUSD office or the Kindergarten Round-Up.

* Submit forms during Open Enrollment to receive priority. Decisions are made during summer.

* A lottery is conducted if there are more requests for a particular school, then space available.

* Families *do not need to reapply* every year for an intradistrict transfer.

Interdistrict

* Pleasanton Residents – Contact the PLUSD to obtain an interdistrict transfer form.

* Non-Pleasanton Residents – Contact your current school district to obtain an interdistrict transfer form. Once Pleasanton residents are placed your child will then be offered a spot if there is space available. A lottery is conducted if there are more requests than space available. Families must reapply annually.

San Leandro

San Leandro Unified School District (SLUSD)
14735 Juniper Street
San Leandro, CA 94579
(510)667-3500
www.sanleandro.k12.ca.us

Elementary School Facts

Schools
* 8 elementary schools are Kindergarten through 5th grade.

* Garfield Elementary is on a year round schedule.

* Placement is determined by home address.

Kindergarten Schedule
* Kindergarten schedules vary across schools. Some schools offer both morning and afternoon schedules while others offer early morning, later morning and afternoon classes.

* A typical kindergarten day is approximately 3.5 hours long.

School Visits
* A kindergarten orientation is typically held in March. In the past the superintendent and school principals are available to answer questions and provide information.

* Contact individual schools to set up a tour.

Before & After Care
* Some schools offer *After-school Clubs of Enrichment* (ACE) a fee-based program. Contact your neighborhood school to learn more.

Busing
- ✶ Special needs students only.

Registration & Enrollment

Dates & Deadlines
- ✶ Registration takes place between March and May.

- ✶ Families who correctly complete and return documents during the Open Enrollment period receive priority.

Process & Procedures
- ✶ Registration takes place onsite at the elementary school.

Documents **Bring original documents**
- ✶ 3 proofs of residency required, acceptable documents include:
  - ↳ Rental agreement or most recent mortgage payment.

  - ↳ 2 utility bills (e.g., PG&E, EBMUD, cable, garbage); SLUSD *does not accept cell phone bills.*

- ✶ Picture ID of parent or legal guardian.

- ✶ Proof of Age (e.g., birth certificate).

- ✶ Proof of Immunizations (yellow card).

- ✶ Proof of Health Exam form completed by physician or medical professional.

- ✶ Proof of Oral Health Exam form completed by dentist.

Transfers

Intradistrict—San Leandro Residents Only
- ✶ Contact the SLUSD Student Support Services department and request an intradistrict transfer.

* Intradistrict transfers decisions are made by school principals typically in June. A lottery is conducted if more requests are made than space available.

* Families need to reapply annually.

Interdistrict

* San Leandro Residents – Contact the SLUSD to obtain an interdistrict transfer form.

* Non-San Leandro Residents – Contact your current school district to obtain an interdistrict transfer form. Forms are due to the SLUSD Student Support Services department in early May. School principals review and make transfer decisions. Families must reapply every year.

San Lorenzo

San Lorenzo Unified School District (SLZUSD)
15510 Usher Street
San Lorenzo, CA 94580
(510)317-4600
www.slzusd.org

Elementary School Facts

Schools
- ✽ 9 elementary schools are Kindergarten through 5th grade.
- ✽ Placement is determined by home address.

Kindergarten Schedule
- ✽ ~8:00 AM to 2:00 PM

School Visits
- ✽ Contact individual schools to set up a tour.

Before & After Care
- ✽ The Boys & Girls Club (510)828-5965 and Adventure Time (www.adventure-time.com) offer after school programs at some of the elementary schools within the San Lorenzo Unified School District.

Busing
- ✽ The SLZUSD provides busing for a fee to elementary school students who are residents of San Lorenzo and live more than 1 ¼ mile from their neighborhood school. To learn more, contact (510)317-4857 or (510)317-4851.

Registration & Enrollment

Dates & Deadlines
* ✶ Registration packets are available in April.

* ✶ Kindergarten Open Enrollment is typically held April through August.

Process & Procedures
* ✶ Registration takes place onsite at the elementary school.

Documents **Bring original documents****
* ✶ 2 proofs of residency are required. According to the district website, *"the district requires verification of residence from families of all students entering grade six and grade nine."* It is not clear if proof of residency is required for kindergarten. In the event that it is, the following have been listed as acceptable documents by the SLZUSD:
  * ↳ Rental agreement or escrow papers.

  * ↳ Current utility bill (PG&E, telephone, cable or EBMUD).

  * ↳ Social service statement showing the name of the student and name and address of parents.

* ✶ Picture ID of parent or legal guardian.

* ✶ Proof of Age (e.g., birth certificate).

* ✶ Proof of Immunizations (yellow card).

* ✶ Proof of Health Exam form completed by physician or medical professional.

* ✶ Proof of Oral Health Exam form completed by dentist.

Transfers

Intradistrict — San Lorenzo Residents Only

✳ Make your intradistrict transfer request in writing during Open Enrollment and turn it in to your resident school.

✳ A lottery is conducted after the Open Enrollment period if there are more requests for a particular school, then school availability.

✳ According to the SLZUSD website, *"Parents of kindergarten students will be notified by the third day of school whether or not their children have been accepted into the school they have requested. Any questions regarding open enrollment should be directed toward the principal of the school of residence."*

Interdistrict

✳ <u>San Lorenzo Residents</u> – Contact the SLZUSD to obtain an interdistrict transfer form.

✳ <u>Non-San Lorenzo Residents</u> – Contact your current school district to obtain an interdistrict transfer form. Once San Lorenzo residents are placed your child will then be offered a spot if there is space available. A lottery will be conducted if there are more requests than space available. Families must reapply every year.

Sunol

Sunol Glen School District (SGSD)
11601 Main Street
Sunol, CA 94586
(925)862-2026
www.sunol.k12.ca.us

Elementary School Facts

Schools
* 1 elementary school is Kindergarten through 8th grade.
* Placement is determined by home address.
* Occasionally SGSD has combined the Kindergarten and 1st grade classes, depending on the number of incoming students.

Kindergarten Schedule
* Morning ~8:30 AM to 11:50 AM.

School Visits
* Contact the Sunol Glen School to schedule a tour.
* Tours are typically offered in March.

Before & After Care
* Sunol Glen School provides fee-based extended care. Call (925)862-0525 to learn more.

Busing
* Busing is available for a fee to residents of Sunol.

Registration & Enrollment

Dates & Deadlines
* Registration begins in March.

Process & Procedures
* Contact the Sunol Glen School (925)862-2026 to pick up a registration packet.

Documents ****Bring original documents****
* Sunol Glen requires families to provide the SGSD with their home address as proof of residency. Other documents required by the SGSD include:

* Picture ID of parent or legal guardian.

* Proof of Age (e.g., birth certificate).

* Proof of Immunizations (yellow card).

* Proof of Health Exam form completed by physician or medical professional.

* Proof of Oral Health Exam form completed by dentist.

Transfers

Intradistrict—Sunol Glen Residents Only
* Since there is only one elementary school, there are no intradistrict transfers.

Interdistrict
* Sunol Glen Residents – Contact the SGSD to obtain an interdistrict transfer form.

* Non-Sunol Glen Residents – Contact your current school district to obtain an interdistrict transfer form. After Sunol Glen residents are placed the superintendent will review applications. Families are typically notified by the end of June. Families must reapply every year.

Union City

New Haven Unified School District (NHUSD)
34200 Alvarado Niles Road
Union City, CA 94587
(510)471-1100
www.nhusd.k12.ca.us

Elementary School Facts

Schools

* 7 elementary schools are Kindergarten through 5th grade.

* NHUSD also provides a home school support program for Kindergarten through 10th grade. Contact the Centralized Enrollment Center at (510)471-1100 x 2318 or Program Manager and teacher, Mrs. Paula Clarke, (510)471-5363 x 2048 to learn more.

* Placement is determined by home address.

Kindergarten Schedule

* Morning ~8:30 AM to Noon

* Afternoon ~Noon to 3:30 PM

* Pioneer School is *piloting an all day kindergarten.*

School Visits

* Kindergarten orientations occur in April, May and August.

* Contact individual schools to set up a tour.

Before & After Care

* Kids First is a fee based onsite extended care program. Contact your home school to learn more.

Busing
- The NHUSD provides busing to residents for a fee. Elementary age students must live more than 3/4 of a mile from school. To learn more, contact the NHUSD website (listed above) or the Transportation Department, at (510)471-5559.

- Applications are available at all school sites. According to the NHUSD website, *"City buses also serve many of the District's attendance areas. For information on city bus schedules, call Union City Transit at (510)471-1411."*

Registration & Enrollment

Dates & Deadlines
- Registration packets are available in March.

Process & Procedures
- Registration and enrollment are centralized and conducted by the district, not by the individual schools.

- 🖐 According to the New Haven Unified School District website,

  The New Haven Unified School District is adopting new boundaries that will determine where elementary students will attend school after Cabello Elementary closes at the end of the current school year and after Barnard-White Middle closes at the end of 2008-09. With the changes, the District anticipates an increased number of requests for intra-district transfers from families assigned to a new home school.

Documents ****Bring original documents****
- 5 proofs of residency are required, acceptable documents include:

↳ Driver's License (with current address) or DMV receipt (if new address). *DMV brown card will not be accepted.*

↳ Closing escrow-papers, mortgage book or statement, rental agreement, or homeowner's association fees statement.

↳ 3 utility (PG&E, EBMUD, cable, telephone, garbage) or credit card bills, or bank statements.

AND any 2 of the following documents:

↳ U.S. Post Office confirmation letter (if new address), current tax return summary page (blank out the dollar amounts), pay stub for prior pay period (blank out the dollar amount), vehicle registration notification letter, any current mail sent from a state or government office (i.e., welfare check, court documents, social security payment, etc.)

* Picture ID of parent or legal guardian.

* Proof of Age (e.g., birth certificate).

* Proof of Immunizations (yellow card).

* Proof of Health Exam form completed by physician or medical professional.

* Proof of Oral Health Exam form completed by dentist.

Transfers

Intradistrict—Union City Residents Only

* Contact the NHUSD offices and request an intradistrict transfer.

* A lottery is conducted if there are more requests for a particular school, then space available.

* Families do not need to reapply every year.

* 🖐 *New boundaries have been drawn* see *Process & Procedures* listed above.

Interdistrict
* Union City Residents – Contact the NHUSD to obtain an interdistrict transfer form.

* Non-Union City Residents – Contact your current school district to obtain an interdistrict transfer form. Once Union City residents are placed your child will then be offered a spot if there is space available. Families must reapply every year.

Choosing a School

March is a hectic time of year for both public and private schools. Many families are anxious to reach the finish line and go back to life before the kindergarten hunt. Take heart, your journey is almost complete. In this chapter we will discuss the final decision making process. Below is a description of how public and private schools handle notification and enrollment. We will conclude with a brief discussion on decision making etiquette.

How Schools Notify Families

Parochial & Non-EBISA Independent Schools

Parochial and non-EBISA independent schools typically make their admissions decisions in spring, usually March. Signing a contract and paying a deposit secures a place for your child. If you have any outstanding questions or concerns address them with the admissions staff prior to signing your contract. If possible and if you feel it necessary, consider requesting another school tour. Contact your target schools directly to learn more about individual school time frames and the decision process.

Independent Schools

Schools belonging to the East Bay Independent Schools Association (EBISA) have agreed to adhere to the same time line when it comes to sending out decision letters. These letters are mailed to families in March, typically on the second Friday of the month. Families are also notified about financial aid awards at this time. The week after decision letters are sent is referred to as, *Quiet Week*. EBISA schools do not contact families during Quiet Week. Their intent is to respect your privacy as you and your family contemplate this important decision. However, admissions staff strongly encourage you to contact them. They are available to answer questions, meet one-on-one, and in some cases offer additional school tours. Take advantage of this opportunity. The staff provide this service as a means of helping you make your decision. If you are offered a spot at an EBISA school, **you will have only one week to make a decision**. Giving a school the official thumbs up requires you to sign a contract and pay a deposit to secure a spot for your child within the one week time frame. If you do not sign the contract and pay the deposit, your spot will be given to the next person on the waiting list.

Public Schools: Alameda County

For many public schools, registration begins and in some cases, ends in March. Some public school districts make an effort to coincide their registration and school assignment process with their local private schools. Intradistrict transfer decisions take place *after* the initial school assignments have been made, typically late spring or summer. Subsequently, interdistrict transfer assignments are not made until after all district residents are placed, typically in late summer or a few days or sometimes weeks into the school year. Refer to TRANSFERS in the PUBLIC SCHOOL section to learn more. In addition, district QUICK FACTS provide a general idea on time frames for each public school district within Alameda County. **Contact your target schools directly to obtain specific dates.**

Types of Decision Letters

All private schools send out decision letters. Public schools typically do not send out decision letters unless they need to conduct a lottery (e.g., all school assignment, overload, transfer). If you have correctly completed and turned in all of your paperwork and space is available, your child is officially enrolled in your public school. In most cases, schools send out one of three types of decision letters. Following is a brief description of each type of letter and some thoughts on how to proceed.

Acceptance

Congratulations! You have worked hard and it has paid off. If your family decides that this is *the* school, then complete and turn in your final paper work. **Receipt of an acceptance letter does not automatically enroll your child at a particular school. Families must notify the school according to the process outlined in your acceptance letter.** Private schools require a signed contract and payment of a deposit to secure a spot for your child. Public schools require the completion and receipt of final registration paper work. Take careful note of where this paperwork needs to be returned, in some cases the documents must go to the district and in others it must be turned in directly to the school site. If your child has been enrolled or offered a spot at another school (private or public) contact the admissions staff immediately so they can make an offer to the next family on their waiting list.

Waiting List

If you receive a letter indicating your child has been placed on the waiting list, call the school immediately. If you and your mates still desire a spot at this school, then find out where your child is on the list and if possible, your chances of obtaining a spot. Keep in touch daily for updates on your child's progress. For whatever reason, if you and your mates do not desire a spot at this school, contact the school immediately and ask to be taken off the list.

Denial

Letters of denial are typically due to three reasons, your child is: 1) eligible but too far down on the waiting list; 2) not ready to begin kindergarten; or 3) not a good match, known as goodness of fit (private school only). Contact the schools or district directly to find out why you were denied. Following is some advice on how to deal with these types of denial.

* *Long Waiting List* - Talk with staff and see what you can do about getting on the waiting list even if it is yards long. What do you have to lose? If you succeed in getting on the list, follow the instructions outlined above in WAITING LIST.

* *Readiness* - The admissions staff believe your child needs another year of preschool, this is not uncommon. Kindergarten is very different from when we attended. Ask the staff for feedback on what specifically makes your child not ready. This information can be helpful if you choose to wait another year for kindergarten.

* *Goodness of Fit* - I realize this may be difficult but try not to take this news personally. School staff usually have a good idea of who will and will not thrive at their school. I encourage you to talk with the admissions staff and get specifics as to why they believe your child is not a good match. This information can be helpful in finding the best school for your child.

Decisions, Decisions: The Final Four

For many families, once the decision letters start rolling in the decision process is rather clear, often the decision is made for them. However there are just as many families where deciding on a school is agonizingly unclear. I have listed below questions to get you and your mates working towards making that final decision.

1. Will my child thrive at this school? Can you picture your little munchkin happy and content at this school or anxious and overwhelmed?

2. How is the commute to this school? Will we be trapped in gridlock for an hour each day or is it a short skateboard ride down the street? A challenging commute is worth it for the right school.

3. Can we afford this school? Keep in mind that private school tuition, without fail, rises annually.

4. What are our feelings about this school? Is there something about this school that makes me, my mates or my child uncomfortable? Do we all feel happy and content with this school?

By all means, if you are feeling wishy washy, contact the school, talk to staff, request another visit, ask more questions, talk with school parents, and if possible, attend one or more school events. Do what you can to help you and your mates work towards making a decision. Following are some scenarios of the decision making process and some advice to help you through it. Keep in mind that everyone's situation is different and therefore these are general responses to get you thinking and working towards making a decision.

What if we are wait-listed at our top school but accepted into another school?

This is tricky. First, contact your top school and explain your situation. They may be able to give you an idea of your chances of moving off of the waiting list. Next, contact school staff at the school where you have been accepted. Address any concerns you have about this particular school with the staff. Request a visit, attend a school event, do what you can to get a feel for this school, and run through the final four questions (listed above) with your mates. A lot can happen over the course of a few days.

What happens if my child does not get in to any of our target schools?

Your first task is to contact all of your target schools and ask them why your child was not offered a spot (see *Denial* above). This feedback will help you decide what to do next. Below I have listed several things you can do:

* *Waiting list* - If you have not already done so, request that your child remain active on the school's waiting list. Families move or change their minds, or for whatever reason space can open up at a particular school. See TYPES OF DECISION LETTERS: WAITING LIST above.

* *Public school* - Enroll your child in public school. Your child is still eligible to attend public school even if you registered for public school but were denied enrollment in your target school(s) because of overload or a denied transfer. Contact district staff to learn more about your options.

* *Home school* - If you have the means, consider home schooling for at least a year. The Bay Area has many resources and groups that support

home school, refer to HOME SCHOOL in the GETTING STARTED chapter.

✳ *Preschool* - Enroll or have your child remain in preschool. This is especially appealing if one or more of your target schools indicated that your child was not ready for kindergarten. Consider preschools that incorporate kindergarten prep into their curriculum.

What do I do if my mate(s) and I disagree on where to send our child?

Once again we go back to the final four (see above). Discuss with your mates, what is best for your child, what you can afford, any commute challenges, and your gut feelings. There may be other idiosyncratic factors that weigh in to your decision. If you and your mates disagree about any of the big four, then talk over your concerns with school staff and school parents, revisit the school, get a consult with Dr. Phil, just do what you must in order to come to a decision.

Decision Making Etiquette: Some Do's and Don'ts

The following is a list of some final decision making etiquette that I heartily encourage you to abide by. This information was obtained from admissions staff and just makes good sense.

DO contact school staff immediately if you do not plan to accept a spot at their school.

They can then make an offer to another family.

DO work the waiting list.

Stay in regular contact with admissions staff since there is a lot of movement shortly after decision letters are sent and right before school begins.

DO NOT put down a deposit at more than one private school.
You and your mates will be pegged with a bad reputation among school staff. This is considered very poor form especially since this behavior denies families on the waiting list a chance at enrolling into one or more of these schools.

DO contact schools to learn why your child was not offered a spot.
This information can be invaluable, especially if you plan to reapply next year.

Post-Acceptance Paperwork

Once your munchkin is enrolled in kindergarten there will be some final paper shuffling. In addition to the signed contract and deposit, families enrolling in private school will need to provide immunization and physical and oral health documentation. Refer to PUBLIC SCHOOL: REGISTRATION PAPERWORK for more details on these documents. Families enrolled in public school typically need to complete a final registration form right before the school year begins. It is easy to let this type of paperwork slide but do your best to get it done and off your plate, then sit back and relax, take a nice deep breath, your search is over.

So Long, Farewell, Auf Wiedersehen, Goodbye

As the old saying goes, you've come along way baby. Reward yourself, your mates and your child for a job well done. Even if you did not get into your top school you and your mates have concluded a worthy journey. So add that notch to your parental belt, kindergarten and all it's adventures will be starting soon. You can sit tight until middle school or for some of you high school or still a small few of you, college. Good luck on your next parenting adventure and if you feel inspired drop me a line and fill me in on the glories of your hunt. I leave and heave a sigh and say goodbye.

Goodbye,

kindersearch@yahoo.com

About the Author

Carol Verboncoeur is the mother of two children, ages eight and six. She is employed at Gordon Heller Institute, specializing in educational research. She, her husband John and the kids live in Oakland, California.

Appendices

Kindergarten Questions

The following is a sampling of kindergarten admissions questions:

School Philosophy & Mission

How would you describe this school?

What is this school's approach to learning? How would I see that played out in the classroom?

What makes this school stand out from other schools?

What are the strengths of this school?

How can this school improve?

What do you like about this school?

How diverse is this school (ethnically, economically, family make up)?

Are there any changes planned for this school in the near future?

Is the school structure earthquake safe? How secure is the school yard? What type of safety features does this school have?

Students

How many children are assigned to a kindergarten class? What is the maximum number?

What types of students do well at this school? What types of students have difficulties?

Where do the students primarily come from (neighborhood? other neighborhoods or cities?)

How are children screened for learning difficulties?

How are students disciplined? Have students been suspended or expelled? If so, why?

How does this school deal with student conflicts?

How does this school honor their students?

How does this school support students who are having difficulties or working ahead?

Where do graduates of this school attend school?

Parents

How can parents get involved at this school?

How does this school communicate with parents? How can parents contact teachers or staff?

Are there mandatory volunteer hours? If so, what is expected?

What type of fund raising is my family expected to take part in?

Does this school offer hot lunch or some sort of meal plan?

Teachers

How many staff are assigned to a kindergarten classroom and what are their roles (teacher, aide, parent volunteer)? How about in the upper grades?

How many teachers are certified to teach at this school?

What is the turnover rate among teachers?

How many years of teaching experience do each of the kindergarten teachers have?

How many years have the kindergarten teachers been at this school?

How does this school recruit and screen teachers? Are background checks conducted? Please describe how this process is handled?

What is each of the kindergarten teachers' strengths, weaknesses?

Are the kindergarten classrooms run differently or the same? Are certain learners or personalities assigned to a certain teacher/classroom?

What specialists do you have on staff (e.g., learning specialist, counselor, librarian)? Are they part time, full time?

What role does the principal / director have at this school?

Schedule & Curriculum

At what time do classes begin and end?

Does the school have a(an) _____ [library, computer lab, art room, gymnasium, playground, science lab]?

How often do the children use the _____ [library, computer lab, art room, gymnasium, playground, science lab]?

Is there a/an _____ [music, art, theater, foreign language, sports program]?

Describe a typical day for a kindergartener. What classes will she attend?

What kind of field trips do the kindergarteners go on? How about upper classmates? How is field trip transportation handled?

Are kindergarteners given homework? If so, how often and on average how long does it take to complete? How do teachers support students who are having trouble with their homework?

What strategies are used to teach students who are not fluent in English?

Admissions

Is overload an issue at this public school? If so, how can my child avoid being overloaded?

How are prospective kindergarteners evaluated? Describe what happens in the interview/evaluation?

What are common mistakes parents applying to or registering in this school (school district) make?

When do you notify families about acceptance (private school) or placement (public school)?

How can I increase my child's chances of being transferred?

Tuition, Fees & Financial Aid

How much is tuition? How often does tuition increase (e.g., annually, every few years)? How much does it increase (e.g. 6%-8%)?

Is tuition reduced if I have more than one child attending?

What other fees am I required to pay?

On average, how much financial aid is awarded each year?

Approximately, how many families receive financial aid?

Extended Care and Other Extras

Does this school offer hot lunch or some sort of meal plan?

How do students get to school? Is busing available?

Is child care available before or after school? Who sponsors extended care (school? private company?)

What do kids do in before and after care? Is there a structured program?

Who are the staff that provide extended care/camp? What are their backgrounds and qualifications?

Does this school offer summer school/summer camp?

Does this school offer care/camps during holidays?

What enrichment programs are offered? Is there a fee?

Notes

.

.

Doodling

Index

www.ingramcontent.com/pod-product-compliance
Lightning Source LLC
Chambersburg PA
CBHW031258090426
42742CB00007B/510

* 9 7 8 0 6 1 5 1 8 9 7 6 5 *